BUDDHA'S
BOOK OF DAILY
MEDITATIONS

Dear Chax

Hope this book is of some use to
you? Thank you so much for all
the advice and teaching you've given
me over the years, i would like to
keep in contact. And learn some more
meditation soon!

Cheers mate

THE
BUDDHA'S
BOOK OF DAILY
MEDITATIONS

✳

Compiled by
Christopher Titmuss

RIDER
LONDON · SYDNEY · AUCKLAND · JOHANNESBURG

1 3 5 7 9 10 8 6 4 2

First published in 2001 by Rider,
an imprint of Ebury Press, Random House,
20 Vauxhall Bridge Road, London SW1 2SA
www.randomhouse.co.uk
This edition published in 2002

Random House Australia (Pty) Limited
20 Alfred Street, Milsons Point, Sydney,
New South Wales 2061, Australia

Random House New Zealand Limited
18 Poland Road, Glenfield,
Auckland 10, New Zealand

Random House South Africa (Pty) Limited
Endulini, 5A Jubilee Road
Parktown 2193, South Africa

The Random House Group Limited Reg. No. 954009

Papers used by Rider are natural, recyclable products
made from wood grown in sustainable forests.

Printed and bound by Bookmarque, Croydon, Surrey

A CIP catalogue record for this book
is available from the British Library

ISBN 0-7126-0189-9

Contents

Acknowledgements

It was a labour of love to select quotes for *The Buddha's Book of Daily Meditations*. I read the suttas (discourses) and verses of the Buddha contained in around 5,000 pages of translation and explanation of the texts from Pali to English. With so many suttas, it was a fascinating task, and I am full of appreciation for the depth and breadth of the Buddha's understanding of the human experience.

I wish to thank my teachers, Venerable Ajahn Dhammadharo of Supanburi, Thailand and the late Venerable Ajahn Buddhadassa of Chai Ya, Thailand, both of whom paid respect to the original teachings through their noble lives.

Between 1970–76, I was a Buddhist monk in the Theravada tradition in Thailand. In the early 1970s, Vimalo Kulbarz of Germany patiently guided me through the entire body of suttas (discourses of the Buddha) so that I had a genuine context for my classical training in the Dharma and Insight Meditation (Vipassana). I have endeavoured to pass his precision and enthusiasm for the original teachings on to my students.

I wish to express much gratitude to the eminent scholar-monk, Bhikkhu Bodhi of the Buddhist Publication Society in Sri Lanka, for his careful translation and editing of many thousands of suttas into English. Since the 1970s he has engaged selflessly in this painstaking and detailed task of Buddhist scholarship to make the exact words of the Buddha available in the English language. We are deeply indebted. Bhikkhu Bodhi kindly looked at my selections for this book.

Many thanks also to Guy Armstrong, a Dharma teacher and colleague, who reviewed my selections. Guy also shares a deep love of the suttas.

I wish to thank various publishers, dedicated to the Dharma, for their kind permission to reproduce passages from their books. I have listed their names and addresses on a separate page. I also wish to express gratitude to Anne Ashton, my secretary, for scanning or typing passages that I highlighted. I have spent as much time preparing this book as writing a book of similar length. I enjoyed every minute of it.

Many thanks to my mother, late father, Richard Gonsky, Dick St. Ruth, Lord Abbots of the Thai Monastery, Bodh Gaya and Sarnath, Gaia House library, Sharpham Buddhist College library; and to the late Thomas Jost from Germany for his many years of dedicated service to Bodh Gaya.

Much gratitude to Nshorna Titmuss, my daughter, for her presence and support.

May all beings live in peace and harmony
May all beings live wisely
May all beings be enlightened

Introduction

I was delighted when Judith Kendra, Publishing Director of Rider Books at Random House UK, invited me to select 365 pieces for *The Buddha's Book of Daily Meditations*. It is a wonderful opportunity to express my gratitude to one of the most remarkable men who walked on this earth. Among Buddhists and non-Buddhists alike, the Buddha is still the leading voice for living with wisdom and compassion, and for realising an enlightened life.

I regard the Buddha as my teacher, friend and guide. I came across his teachings (the Dharma) in India in 1967. I don't think I've gone a day without feeling blessed at having exposure to the Buddha, the Dharma and the Sangha of men and women committed to the Dharma. During my six years as a Buddhist monk, I received Vipassana training in the Theravada tradition, the oldest of the Buddhist traditions, in Thailand. For the past 25 years, I have considered myself a servant of the Buddha through sharing the Dharma of awakening worldwide.

The beneficial influence of the Buddha falls into three primary areas.

The First Great Benefit – Non-harming

The Buddha spoke tirelessly about engaging in a way of life that resolutely refuses to justify causing harm and suffering to others. Do we support war that generates unimaginable suffering to soldiers, civilians, animals and the environment? Do we deliberately use harsh words designed to hurt the feelings of others? With an impassioned concern, he consistently reminded humanity of our personal responsibility to look at our actions to see what causes suffering.

In a celebrated statement, he said 'I declare there is suffering in this world. I declare there is the resolution of suffering.' In many respects, people haven't changed at all. For countless centuries, everyone has met similar issues in daily life. I realised that wherever we find wisdom, we find the Buddha. The Buddha said that even if someone grabs at his clothes, they do not touch him. 'Only one who sees the Dharma sees the Buddha.'

To understand the Buddha's teachings of non-harming, we need to experience a deep intimacy with others. What the Buddha discovered applies as much today as it did when he was alive. In this intimacy with past, present and future, we experience a profound sense of non-difference. Initially, what we see in others is the interaction of body, speech and mind, just as we experience in ourselves. Nobody is fundamentally different from anybody else. If we truly understand this, we treat others as we wish them to treat us. In deep intimacy, non-harming transforms from an ethical practice into a realisation of oneness in relationship. Whenever we find the heart's expression of a non-harming way of life, we find the Buddha.

The Second Great Benefit – Meditation

The Buddha emphasised the importance of meditation as a vital feature in the range of his teachings. At times, it is hard to imagine how people get by in their daily lives without regular meditation to help them stay grounded in the moment. Authentic meditation examines every area of the inner life. Meditation means to sit, walk, stand, recline, with dedicated attention and clarity in the here and now. The Buddha said that meditation concerns itself with calm and insight (samatha and vipassana; vi -passana = in-seeing). In an exquisite analogy, he said calm and insight are like two birds that fly through windows of the castle. The castle means the body and the sense doors refer to the windows. The two birds bring to awareness (the lord of the castle) the message of liberation.

Through samatha, we discover depths of contentment, peace of mind and opening out of the contracted heart. Through insight, we see into hindrances of the mind, dissolve the power of the ego and get to know ourselves thoroughly. The Buddha makes clear the priority for calm and insight through focused inquiry into the nature of the body, feelings, states of mind and the Dharma of daily life.

The Buddha reminds us that wherever we go in the world, our mind and body go along with us. This is our instrument not only for contact with the world, but also for contact with ourselves. If there is a lack of wisdom in our inner life, we suffer and others suffer. Our brothers and sisters in the Christian tradition point out that there are sins of commission and sins of omission. Sins of commission mean the deliberate attempt to cause others suffering through acts of body, speech and mind. We easily fall prey to such patterns in order to get what we want.

Sins of omission mean that the individual does not intentionally cause suffering but brings it about for others through lack of awareness or neglect.

Empathy for the feelings of others emerges out of deep and regular meditation. We can understand the pain of others, even if it is not our personal experience. True empathy changes behaviour patterns. The Buddha points to awareness and resolution of suffering, intentional and unintentional, as much as possible. In meditation this becomes clear.

Mindfulness and awareness in daily life, along with formal meditation, contribute to a depth of samadhi. There is no equivalent for this word in the English language. It communicates meditative concentration, inner stability, sublime joy and true peace of mind. In samadhi, there is a steadfast focus. One is centred in the here and now. Not surprisingly, the Buddha placed importance on not clinging to events of past, present or future, not grasping experiences, things or situations. Through non-grasping, we experience natural samadhi.

The Third Great Benefit – Wisdom

With regard to his teachings, the Buddha urged followers of the Dharma to use their discernment. He did not want us to agree with his every word. He spoke without fear or favour. The public image that the Buddha was holier-than-thou doesn't fit in with the Buddhist texts, known as the Pali Suttas. At times, he spoke bluntly. When he was offered a woman for pleasure, he described the body as a 'thing full of urine and excrement'. He also spoke with poetic sweetness comparing life to a 'dewdrop on the tip of a blade of grass'.

The Buddha taught a down-to-earth wisdom. He told us to shake off our obsession with the pursuit of pleasure and wake up. He showed no regard for the traditional guru-disciple relationship. He spoke as an adult to adults. He referred to himself as a 'good friend'. It was a revolutionary message calling for revolutionary change in personal, social, religious and political life. For the Buddha, four things mattered – suffering, the causes of suffering, a profound liberation and the way to realise liberation.

The Buddha indicated that right understanding means the problem stands under us and ceases to trouble our minds. To understand is to dissolve wanting and clinging. The inner suffering has then gone. Wisdom enables clear action to be taken as an outcome. In the cessation of suffering and dissatisfaction, there is the knowing of a timeless freedom we cannot measure, that death cannot take away. The Buddha said that this is Nirvana.

Just as the sun shines, whether there are clouds or not, so freedom shines through our variety of experiences. When we live a truly noble way of life, we experience this great liberation from one day to the next. It is not some absolute state to escape into, nor an occasional taste of feeling free when things are going our way.

There is nothing more worthwhile than knowing deep down an enlightened way of being. Nothing in transient existence has the power to take this enlightenment away. In this very life, we can know intimately what the Buddha understood. It is no easy undertaking to end karma conclusively, namely the painful influences upon our inner lives of the past on the present. It is no easy task to explore what it means to lead an utterly fulfilled life without becoming spellbound by religious and scientific beliefs. To step out of the imprisonment of unhealthy and unsatisfactory states of mind marks the standpoint of liberation.

What is enlightenment? It is an umbrella concept referring to knowing a profoundly liberating wisdom. This includes realisation of the Unconditioned (Nirvana, the Deathless, Liberation) that embraces past, present and future. An enlightened one understands the conditions for suffering and the resolution of them. He or she respects and applies the ethics of non-harming, meditation and wisdom.

Deep friendship for all beings fills the heart of the enlightened ones. There is the capacity to stay steady in the midst of pressure, to abide fearlessly in difficult circumstances. Enlightened ones experience absence or virtual absence of problems in their daily lives and much happiness in the ordinary. They reveal a wonderful generosity of spirit.

I believe in the historical person of the Buddha for one reason. The texts show a depth of experience and understanding which in my view would be inaccessible to a thinker, academic or philosopher. The Dharma, that is the teachings and practices to realise an enlightened life, clearly emerges out of profound experiences and insights, not just the result of a clever mind.

My deepest gratitude goes to the Buddhas of past, present and future for pointing out the unsurpassable Dharma that enlightens the lives of humanity.

CHRISTOPHER TITMUSS

Note to Reader

I wish to express my immense gratitude to the tradition of Buddhist monk-scholars of Sri Lanka who have worked tirelessly for years to make the discourses (suttas) of the Buddha available to the English-speaking world. This book would not be possible without their noble work. Such monks, past and present, as Bhikkhu Nanatiloka, Bhikkhu Nanamoli, Bhikkhu Nanaponika, Bhikkhu Narada Thera, Bhikkhu Bodhi and the Buddhist Publication Society of Kandy, Sri Lanka, have contributed significantly to our understanding of the Dharma.

I have selected the most authoritative translations of the suttas available in the English language. I have remained very respectful to these eminent translators. I have made only modest changes, including editing the length of some sentences or making some deletions where there is repetition. It is commonly agreed that some words translated from the Pali are difficult to communicate in English in a single word. At times, English does not have the subtlety of concepts used in Pali to describe this vast field of experience. The Buddha encouraged use of contemporary language and occasionally I have done exactly that.

I have used the more common Sanskrit spelling of Dharma rather than the Pali spelling of Dhamma. At times I have made changes where appropriate. These include:

lust or sense desire *to* pursuit of pleasure, desire for sensual satisfaction,

renunciation *to* giving up, letting go

deliverance *to* freedom

concentration *to* meditative concentration

being *to* becoming

holy life *to* spiritual life

disciples *to* students

dependent origination *to* dependent arising

right view *to* right understanding

Brahmins *to* priests

Voidness *to* Emptiness

Tathagata *to* One Thus Gone (beyond all wanting and clinging; name for a fully liberated one)

I believe such slight changes will help readers to understand the heart of the Buddha's teachings. His words serve as a foundation for one of the world's great religions and, more importantly, he shows humanity the way to end suffering. Readers may regard some of the Buddha's insights as obscure and difficult to comprehend. This will not be the case for everybody, and those who have explored the depths of inner experience, particularly through meditation, will understand them easily. It would water down the teachings to leave out these passages.

It is important to remember that this is a book of meditations. It is not intended as a light read. You may need to read, reflect and meditate upon some extracts from the discourses several times to get a sense of what the Buddha is pointing out. At times, the Buddha observed Noble Silence to communicate profound teachings. The meditation for April 22 consists of a blank page to indicate the inability of words to express the inexpressible.

I wish to express deepest gratitude to Wisdom Publications, the Buddhist publishers of Boston, USA, who kindly gave permission to use quotes from the Middle Length Discourses, Longer Discourses and the Connected Discourses of the Buddha. Some 60 per cent of the quotes in this book come from these three volumes.

Wisdom Publications engaged in an enormous financial undertaking to publish these three books which amount in total to some 4,000 pages of texts. They showed an extraordinary generosity of spirit to give another major publishing house permission to use some 200 quotes from three of the main texts in their catalogue. It reflects their determination to make the precise teachings of the Buddha available to as many people as possible.

Finally, I would like to thank the Pali Text Society of Oxford, England, founded in 1881, whose staff and translators have made available these sacred texts.

This book of daily meditations serves as an introduction to the full discourses. I can only encourage readers of *The Buddha's Book of Daily Meditations* to take the next step and to purchase the comprehensive teachings of the Buddha found in the Middle Length Discourses, Longer Discourses and Connected Discourses of the Buddha. I regard these books as the three jewels of all Buddhist texts. I have written about the heart of the Buddha's teachings, such as the Four Noble Truths and the Eightfold Path, in my previous book *Light on Enlightenment*.

I hope *The Buddha's Book of Daily Meditations* will inspire you to explore further his teachings of awareness, the heart, meditation and an enlightened wisdom.

May all beings live with clarity
May all beings understand the nature of things
May all beings be enlightened.

Outline of the
Discourses of the Buddha

There are more than 5,500 suttas, or discourses, delivered by the Buddha during his forty-five years of teaching. The suttas are grouped into five *nikayas*, or collections:

THE MIDDLE LENGTH DISCOURSES OF THE BUDDHA translated by Bhikkhu Nanamoli and Bhikkhu Bodhi from *Majjhima Nikaya*. 1,232 pages published in 1995 by Wisdom Publications, 199 Elm Street, Somerville, Boston, MA 02144, USA. Tel: 617 776 7410 ext. 40. Website: www.wisdompubs.org. The 'Middle-length' Discourses (Pali *majjhima* = 'middle') consist of 152 suttas.

THE LONG DISCOURSES OF THE BUDDHA translated by Maurice Walshe from the *Digha Nikaya*. 648 pages published in 1995 by Wisdom Publications, 199 Elm Street, Somerville, Boston, MA 02144, USA. The 'Long' Discourses (Pali *digha* = 'long') consist of 34 suttas.

NUMERICAL DISCOURSES OF THE BUDDHA edited and translated by Bhikkhu Bodhi from the *Anguttara-Nikaya*, published in 2000 by Rowman and Littlefield, USA. Original translation by E.M. Hare from five volumes, approximately 1,400 pages, published in 1978 by Pali Text Society and Unwin Brothers Limited, The Gresham Press, Old Woking, Surrey, England. The discourses consist of 2,308 short suttas, grouped together into eleven *nipatas* according to the number of items of Dharma covered in each sutta. For example, the *Eka-nipata* ('Book of the Ones') contains suttas about a single item of Dharma; the *Duka-nipata* ('Book of the Twos') contains suttas dealing with two items of Dharma, and so on.

THE CONNECTED DISCOURSES OF THE BUDDHA translated by Bhikkhu Bodhi from the *Samyutta-Nikaya*. Approximately 2,000 pages, two volumes, published in November 1995 by Wisdom

Publications, 199 Elm Street, Somerville, Boston, MA, 02144, USA. Tel: 617 776 7410 ext. 40. Website: www.wisdompubs.org. This is a collection of thematically-connected short suttas. The discourses consist of 2,889 shorter suttas grouped together into 56 themes.

THE DIVISION OF SHORT BOOKS (Pali *khud.da* = 'smaller') consisting of books shorter in length.

THE SUTTA-NIPATA translated by Venerable Saddhatissa. 135 pages, published in 1985 by Curzon Press Limited, 42 Gray's Inn Road, London WC1, England.

THE DHAMMAPADA (423 verses) translated by Venerable Acharya Buddharakkhita with introduction by Bhikkhu Bodhi, published by the Buddhist Publication Society, Kandy, PO Box 61, 54 Sangharaja Mawatha, Kandy, Sri Lanka.

THE UDANA AND THE ITIVUTTAKA translated by John D. Ireland, published by the Buddhist Publication Society, Kandy, PO Box 61, 54 Sangharaja Mawatha, Kandy, Sri Lanka.

MINOR READINGS translated by Bhikkhu Nanamoli, published by the Pali Text Society, 73 Lime Walk, Headington, Oxford OX3 7AD, England.

More than 700 suttas translated by other monks can be found on the website **www.accesstoinsight.org**

A Short Biography
of the Buddha

In the year 560 BC, Siddhartha Gautama entered this world when he was born to Queen Mahamaya under a tree in a public park in Lumbini, north India. His father, King Suddhodana, the ruler of the Sakyan kingdom, gave him the name Siddhartha which means 'Wish Fulfilled'. Queen Mahamaya died seven days after the birth and Siddhartha was brought up by her sister.

At that time, Hindu society was firmly divided into castes, or social groups. The four main castes were the Brahmins, who held the religious power throughout the country; the Kshatriyas, who were both the ruling class and military class; the Vaishyas, consisting of the business community, and finally the Sudras, or workers. Not long after the birth of Siddhartha, Kondanna, a Brahmin, made a prediction that Siddhartha would either become a great ruler or renounce his responsibilities within the ruling class and pursue enlightenment.

By all accounts, Siddhartha led a very sheltered life. The royal family protected him from any kind of real exposure to suffering and anguish. He was always kept at a distance from such suffering so that the royal household could ensure he sustained a privileged and aloof view of society. On a trip into the countryside with Channa, his charioteer, Siddhartha saw a very old man with 'no teeth, sunken cheeks, dry skin, wrinkles, bleary eyes and bent back'.

Then he saw a very sick person lying on the ground, groaning in agony. Next Siddhartha observed a funeral where the mourners were weeping and crying as they carried the lifeless body to the cremation ground. He turned to Channa in utter despair: 'Must everyone I love and myself too simply endure helplessly this tyranny of old age, sickness and death?'

Later, on another trip, he spotted a wandering sage who had

renounced the conventional lifestyle to seek wisdom and liberation through simplicity of living and meditation. Siddhartha found himself plunged into depression, turmoil and inner conflict. He lost all interest in his way of life, in living in a world of pleasure and becoming the future King of the Sakyan people.

One night there was yet another major royal function with food, music, dancing, and lavish entertainment for the ruling class. He hated the event and made the decision to run away. That night, upon returning to the palace, he decided that he would abandon all of his duties as a prince, husband and father and try to find a way out of his turmoil. Yet only seven days previously, Siddhartha had become a father when his wife, Princess Yasodhara, the most beautiful woman of the kingdom, gave birth to their son, Rahula.

Haunted by the prospect of having to face ageing, sickness and death, Siddhartha felt the longer his life went on the worse the horror would be. He lost all appetite for wealth, fame and his legendary handsome presence. He regarded them as three terrible karmas. Siddhartha said to himself, 'I must go without seeing my son's face. When I have resolved this suffering I am going through and found a way out of ageing, sickness and death, I shall immediately return to tell Yasodhara and Rahula what I have found.'

Channa took him to the edge of the city where he removed his silk clothes, jewellery and sword and handed these items to his charioteer. He put on some old garments, cut his long hair short and set off walking through the night as the first steps to finding himself and facing up to existence.

For the next six years, Siddhartha spent his time engaged in a whole variety of religious and aesthetic practices to overcome his fears about life. He felt determined to find a genuine liberation that would dissolve the hold over his life of impermanence. He spent time with a celebrated spiritual teacher named Alara Kalama who pointed to a state of Infinite Nothingness as the escape from the world of change and death. Alara invited Siddhartha to teach with him since he also reached that state. Siddhartha realised that he could enter this state through meditation but then would have to go back into the world of suffering.

He then went to visit another famous teacher of meditation called Uddaka Ramaputta. He had gone a step further than Alara Kalama but still Siddhartha knew that Uddaka had not found the fulfilment of the spiritual life. He then pursued his own way. Along with five others he stayed in a hermitage in Sarnath, previously called Uruvela, where they engaged in severe austerities, especially fasting, to overcome any lingering attachment to the body.

Siddhartha gave up trying to rid himself of attachment to the body through this means, left his aesthetic friends and walked for some weeks to another part of the country. He arrived in the village of Bodh Gaya feeling tired and weak. A young woman, named Sujata, saw his condition and offered him a bowl of rice milk. Gaining strength, he spent yet another night in meditation, under a sacred tree beside a nearby river called Neranjara, in one final attempt to awaken fully.

During the night, he recalled sitting under a tree in a field at the age of twelve. He remembered the joy, contentment and calm inner absorption he felt at that time. Now, at the age of thirty-five, he allowed himself to feel that joy once again. During the night, he became exposed to a variety of meditation experiences and then he realised the struggle that human beings face day in and day out. He saw the way people get caught up in their suffering and the conditions leading to that. He realised the dissolution of these conditions and the way for that to happen. All of this became utterly clear to him. He felt an incredible release. He had finally woken up.

He had overcome his inner struggle to make sense of a life that pursued pleasure and privilege to escape the harsh realities of existence. That world of indulging in pleasure and fearing pain totally lost its hold over his existence. He was awake. He was liberated. In addition, he knew that this awakening was available to everybody with the interest and quiet determination to look into the core issues of living.

Siddhartha stayed in the village for the next seven weeks, reflecting on what he had realised. He then made the 170-mile walk back to Sarnath to speak with his friends about his awakening. He explained to them that the extremes of self-hatred and self-gratification inhibited the opportunity for an awakened life.

He then set off to Kapilavastu to see Yasodhara, his wife, and Rahula, his six-year-old son, to tell them that his inner turmoil and depression were completely over. He had discovered the Deathless nature of things so that ageing, sickness and death had ceased to be an issue for him any more. From the time of reconnecting with his son, the Buddha remained a devoted father. The texts record a number of talks with his son on spiritual practice.

From that time on until his death at the age of 80, he walked throughout north India giving teachings and practices to tens of thousands of men, women and children that pointed to a truly liberated and enlightened life. Siddhartha came to be known throughout the region as the 'Awakened One' (the Buddha). Yasodhara and Rahula accompanied him on his long walks with other friends to cities, towns and villages in that region to teach the Dharma of liberation.

Siddhartha died under a tree in Kushinagara after he had eaten some poisonous mushrooms. During his last night on earth, a man came to him to ask him about how he would be able to identify an enlightened teacher. The Buddha advised the man not to concern himself with searching for an enlightened teacher but instead to devote himself to the Dharma of awareness into body, feelings, states of mind and Dharma practices to discover an enlightened life. The Buddha advised the man to work out his liberation with diligence.

Thus ended the life of one of the most remarkable men to have lived on this earth. His voice for a fully enlightened life embraced morality, inquiry, depth of meditation, insight, compassion and a liberating wisdom. Ever since, he has struck a strong cord with count-less men and women determined to see through their own experience to what matters most deeply.

The core of his teachings has as much relevance today as it did 2,500 years ago.

May all beings see into the nature of things
May all beings be awakened
May all beings be fully liberated

THE
BUDDHA'S
BOOK OF DAILY
MEDITATIONS

JANUARY 1

❋

The spiritual life does not have gain, honour and fame for its goal, or the attainment of virtue or the attainment of meditative concentration or knowledge and vision. But unshakeable freedom of mind is the goal of the spiritual life.

JANUARY 2

❋

Whatever should be done by a compassionate teacher who, out of compassion, seeks the welfare of his students, that I have done for you. These are the roots of trees, these are empty huts. Meditate, do not be negligent, lest you regret it later. This is our instruction to you.

JANUARY 3

❋

Hatred never ceases by hatred in this world; hatred ceases through non-hatred. This is an endless truth.

JANUARY 4

✳

One acts in full awareness when eating, drinking, consuming food and tasting. One acts in full awareness when defaecating and urinating. One acts in full awareness when walking, standing, sitting, falling asleep, waking up, talking and keeping silent.

JANUARY 5

❋

When one is liberated, one knows three unsurpassable qualities: unsurpassable vision, unsurpassable practice and unsurpassable freedom. The Buddha teaches Nirvana and he teaches the Dharma for attaining Nirvana.

JANUARY 6

*

These eight worldly conditions keep the world turning around, and the world turns around these eight worldly conditions. What eight?

Gain and loss,

Success and failure,

Praise and blame,

Pleasure and pain.

They are encountered by an uninstructed worldling, and they are also encountered by an instructed noble student. When an uninstructed worldling comes upon gain, he does not reflect on it thus: 'This gain that has come to me is impermanent, bound up with suffering, subject to change.' He does not know it as it really is. Being thus involved in likes and dislikes, he will not be free from suffering.

An instructed noble student reflects thus: 'This gain that has come to me is impermanent, bound up with suffering, subject to change.' He understands all these things as they really are, and they do not engross his mind.

JANUARY 7

❉

We will guard the doors of our sense faculties. On seeing a form with the eye, we will not grasp at its signs and features. If we left the eye faculty unguarded, unwholesome states of envy and grief might invade us. We will practise the way of its restraint.

JANUARY 8

*

One who looks upon the world as a bubble and a
mirage, the King of Death does not see.

JANUARY 9

❋

Suppose a man were to take a loan and his business were to succeed so that he could repay all the money of the old loan and there would remain enough extra to maintain a wife; then on considering this, he would be glad and full of joy.

Or suppose a man was sent to prison but later he would be released safe and secure, with no loss to his property; then on considering this, he would be glad and full of joy.

So too, when mental hindrances (greed, anger, boredom, worry, doubt) have been abandoned, he experiences that in the same way as freedom from debt or a release from prison.

JANUARY 10

❋

There are two conditions for the arising of right understanding: the voice of another and wise attention. Right understanding is assisted by five factors when it has liberation by wisdom for its fruit, namely morality, reflection, discussion, calmness and insight.

JANUARY 11

＊

There are four ways of undertaking things. What are the four?

There is a way of undertaking things that is pleasant now and ripens in the future as pain.

There is the way of undertaking things that is painful now and ripens in the future as pain.

There is the way of undertaking things that is painful now and ripens in the future as pleasant.

There is the way of undertaking things that is pleasant now and ripens in the future as pleasant.

JANUARY 12

✳

If there were no Unborn, Unbecoming, Unmade, Unconditioned, no way out would be discerned from what is born, has become, made and conditioned. But since there is an Unborn, Unbecoming, Unmade and Unconditioned, there is a way out.

JANUARY 13

❋

He abides pervading one quarter with a mind imbued with loving-kindness, likewise the second, likewise the third, likewise the fourth; so above, below, around and everywhere.

And to all, as to himself, he abides pervading the all-encompassing world with a mind imbued with loving-kindness, abundant, exalted, immeasurable, without hostility and without ill will.

❋

It is by living close to a person that his morality is to be known. Then only after a long time, not after a short period; and only by considering that person, not without consideration; and only by one who is wise, not by a fool.

It is by associating with a person that his clarity is to be known.

It is in adversity that a person's fortitude is to be known.

It is by discussion with a person that his wisdom is to be known and then only after a long time, not after a short period.

JANUARY 15

❋

Having abandoned formal religious practices altogether and actions both 'good' and 'bad', neither longing for 'purity' nor 'impurity', one wanders aloof, abstaining from both without adhering to either extreme.

JANUARY 16

✳

In every direction there are things you know and recognise, above, below, around and within. Leave them: do not look to them for rest or relief, do not let consciousness dwell on the products of existence, on things that come and go.

JANUARY 17

*

Dry up the remains of your past and have nothing for your future. If you do not cling to the present then you can go from place to place in peace.

19

JANUARY 18

✳

Udaya asked: 'How does the mindful person bring his mind-flow to an end?'

'The sensations that you feel from the inside have no more fascination for you. And the sensations that you feel from the outside no longer fascinate you. Such a person is mindful and brings his mind-flow to an end.'

JANUARY 19

❉

Where neither water nor yet earth
Nor fire nor air gain a foothold,
There gleam no stars, no sun sheds light,
There shines no moon,
Yet there no darkness reigns.
When one has come to know this
For oneself, through one's own wisdom,
Then there is freedom from form and formless.

*

To avoid all evil, to cultivate good and to purify one's mind – this is the teaching of the Buddhas.

JANUARY 21

❋

There is no meditative concentration for him who lacks insight, and no insight for him who lacks meditative concentration. One who experiences both meditative concentration and insight is indeed close to Nirvana.

JANUARY 22

❋

Talk that is a help in opening up the mind, and which conduces to complete turning away, peace, direct knowing, enlightenment and Nirvana – that is:

Talk about fewness of wishes,

Talk about contentment,

Talk about seclusion,

Talk about putting forth energy,

Talk about morality,

Talk about meditative concentration,

Talk about liberation,

Talk about the knowledge and vision of liberation.

JANUARY 23

❋

Not understanding thoughts,
One runs back and forth with wandering mind.

＊

Though all his life a fool associates with a wise person, he no more comprehends the Truth than a spoon tastes the flavour of the soup.

JANUARY 25

❋

One is the quest for wordly gain, and quite another is the path to enlightenment. Clearly understanding this, let not a student of the Buddha be carried away by worldly acclaim, but develop non-attachment instead.

JANUARY 26

❋

Neither mother, father, nor any other relative can do
one greater good than one's own well-directed mind.

JANUARY 27

*

Those whose minds have reached full excellence in the factors of enlightenment, who, having renounced acquisitiveness, rejoice in not clinging to things – glowing with wisdom, they have attained Nirvana in this very life.

JANUARY 28

✴

There are two kinds of happiness: the kind to be pursued and the kind to be avoided. When I observed that in the pursuit of such happiness, unwholesome factors increased and wholesome factors decreased, then that happiness was to be avoided.

When I observed that in the pursuit of such happiness unwholesome factors decreased and wholesome ones increased, then that happiness was to be sought after.

Now, there is happiness accompanied by pondering, and happiness not accompanied by it. Of the two, the latter is more excellent. This leads to the cessation of the tendency to project and conceptual proliferation.

✳

It is just as if a man were to say: 'I am going to seek out and love the most beautiful girl in the country.' They might say to him: 'Well, as to this most beautiful girl in the country, do you know whether she belongs to the military, the priestly, the business or the working class?'

He would say: 'No.' Then they might say: 'Well, do you know her name, her family, whether she is tall, short or of medium height, dark, light-complexioned or sallow-skinned, or what village, town or city she comes from?' and he would say: 'No.'

They might say: 'Well then, you don't know or see the one you seek for and desire?' and he would say: 'No.' Does not the talk of that man turn out to be stupid?

The questioner replied: 'Certainly.'

'So it is with those who declare and believe that after death the self is entirely happy and free from disease. Does not their talk turn out to be stupid (since it is an only a claim)?'

'Certainly.'

JANUARY 30

❋

Riches ruin only the foolish, not those in quest of the Beyond. By craving for riches the witless person ruins himself as well as others.

JANUARY 31

*

What is the Noble Truth of the Way of Practice leading to the Cessation of Suffering? It is just this Noble Eightfold Path, namely:

Right Understanding

Right Intention

Right Speech

Right Action

Right Livelihood

Right Effort

Right Mindfulness

Right Meditative Concentration

FEBRUARY 1

٭

What is suffering? Birth is suffering; ageing is suffering; sickness is suffering; death is suffering; sorrow, lamentation, pain, grief, and despair are suffering; not getting what one wants is suffering; losing what one has is suffering; being separated from who and what one loves is suffering. In short, the five aggregates (body, feelings, perceptions, thoughts, consciousness) affected by clinging are suffering.

FEBRUARY 2

✳

What are causes of suffering? It is craving, which brings renewal of becoming, is accompanied by infatuation and lust for this and that. There is craving for sensual pleasures, craving for becoming and craving for not becoming.

FEBRUARY 3

✳

What is the cessation of suffering? It is the fading away and ceasing, the giving up and letting go of that same craving. This is called the cessation of suffering.

FEBRUARY 4

❋

What is Right Understanding? It is the knowledge of suffering, the knowledge of the causes of suffering, the knowledge of the cessation of suffering and the knowledge of the way of practice leading to the cessation of suffering.

FEBRUARY 5

❋

What is Right Intention? The intention of letting go,
the intention for the absence of ill-will, the intention
for the absence of harm.

FEBRUARY 6

✳

What is Right Speech? Refraining from lying, refraining from slander, refraining from harsh speech, refraining from frivolous speech.

FEBRUARY 7

*

What is Right Action? Refraining from taking life, refraining from taking what is not given, refraining from sexual misconduct. This is called Right Action.

FEBRUARY 8

❋

What is Right Effort? Here, one rouses one's intention, stirs up energy, exerts one's mind and strives to prevent the arising of unarisen evil or unwholesome mental states.

One exerts one's mind to overcome evil or unwholesome mental states that have arisen.

One exerts one's mind to cultivate unarisen wholesome mental states.

One exerts one's mind to maintain wholesome mental states that have arisen, not to let them fade away, to bring them to greater growth, to fulfillment of development.

FEBRUARY 9

❋

What is Right Mindfulness?

One abides contemplating body as body, ardent,
clearly aware and mindful, having put aside
hankering and fretting for the world.

One abides contemplating feelings as feelings.

One abides contemplating states of mind as states
of mind.

One abides contemplating Dharma as Dharma,
ardent, clearly aware and mindful, having put aside
longing and worrying about the world.

FEBRUARY 10

❋

What is Right Meditative Concentration?

Secluded from sensual pleasures, secluded from unwholesome states, one enters upon and abides in the first meditative absorption, which is accompanied by applied and sustained reflection, with joy and happiness born of seclusion.

   With the subsiding of applied and sustained reflection, by gaining inner calmness and oneness of mind, one enters and remains in the second meditative absorption, born of meditative concentration filled with joy and happiness.

✳

With the fading away of delight, remaining imperturbable, mindful and clearly aware, he experiences in himself the joy of which the Noble Ones say: 'Happy is he who dwells with equanimity and mindfulness', he enters the third meditative absorption.

Having given up pleasure and pain, and with the disappearance of former gladness and sadness, he enters and remains in the fourth meditative absorption which is beyond pleasure and pain, and purified by equanimity and mindfulness.

FEBRUARY 12

❋

There are four kinds of verbal conduct not in accordance with the Dharma. Here someone speaks falsehood; when summoned to a court, a meeting, his relatives' presence, royal family's presence, and questioned as a witness. thus:

Not knowing, he says, 'I know'.

Or knowing, he says, 'I do not know';

Not seeing, he says, 'I see'.

Or seeing, he says, 'I do not see'.

He speaks falsehood for his own ends, or for another's ends, or for some worldly end.

FEBRUARY 13

❋

These five trades should not be taken up:

trading with weapons,

trading in living beings,

trading in meat,

trading in intoxicants,

trading in poison.

FEBRUARY 14

❋

He who calls others 'a fool' and 'holder of impure Dharma' would indeed invite strife.

FEBRUARY 15

✳

When he does not think, 'This is mine' or 'That belongs to them', then, since he has no egoism, he cannot grieve with the thought of 'I do not have'.

❋

'What is it', said Ajita, 'that smothers the world? What makes the world so hard to see? What would you say pollutes the world, and what threatens it most?'

'It is ignorance that smothers the world. It is carelessness and greed that make the world invisible. The hunger of desire pollutes the world, and the fear of the pain of suffering threatens it.'

FEBRUARY 17

✳

When a person has assessed the world from top to bottom, when there is nothing in the world that raises a flicker of agitation, then he has become a person free from the tremblings and the hunger of desire. He has become calm. He has gone beyond getting old.

FEBRUARY 18

❋

When a person has gone beyond, then there is nothing by which you can measure him or her. That by which he can be talked about is no longer there for him. Yet you cannot say that he does not exist.

All ways of description have been removed.

FEBRUARY 19

❋

'I do not say that religious teachers and priests are wrapped in the shroud of birth and ageing,' said the Buddha.

'There are some who have let go of world-views. They have let go of religious practices and rituals, they have left all the different forms behind and they have a total understanding of attachments.

'For them there are no inner poison-drives. These, truly, are the ocean-crossers.'

FEBRUARY 20

❋

There is nothing that you need hold on to and there is nothing that you need push away.

FEBRUARY 21

❀

There is, in taking things, a thirst, a clinging, a grasping. You must lose it. You must lose it altogether,
above, below, around and within. It makes no
difference what it is you are grasping at: when you
grasp, Mara (the Force of Temptation) stands beside
you.

FEBRUARY 22

❋

If you are always aware, you will look at the world and see its emptiness. If you give up looking at yourself as a fixed and special identity, then you will have given yourself a way to go beyond death.

Look at the world like this and the King of Death will not see you.

FEBRUARY 23

❀

This being, that is; from the arising of this, that arises.
That is:

With ignorance as condition, volitional activities
come to be;

With volitional activities as condition, consciousness
comes to be;

With consciousness as condition, name-and-form
comes to be;

With name-and-form as condition, the sixfold base
comes to be;

With the sixfold sense base as condition, contact
comes to be;

With contact as condition, feeling comes to be;

With feeling as condition, craving comes to be;

With craving as condition, grasping comes to be;

With grasping as condition, becoming comes to be;

With becoming as condition, birth comes to be;

With birth as condition, ageing and death, sorrow,
lamentation, pain, grief and despair come to be.

This is the origin of this whole mass of suffering.

FEBRUARY 24

✳

This not being, that is not; from the cessation of this, that ceases.

FEBRUARY 25

❋

Not by water is one purified,
Many people bathe in water to be purified.
In whom is Truth and Dharma,
One is purified.

❋

Herein you should train yourself thus: 'In the seen will be merely what is seen; in the heard will be merely what is heard; in the sensed will be merely what is sensed; in the knowing will be merely what is knowing. Then there will be no here nor there nor in-between. This is the end of suffering.'

FEBRUARY 27

*

Rahula,

Develop meditation on loving kindness for ill-will will be abandoned

Develop meditation on compassion for any cruelty will be abandoned

Develop meditation on appreciative joy for any discontent will be abandoned

Develop meditation on equanimity for any aversion will be abandoned

Develop meditation on foulness for any lust will be abandoned

Develop meditation on the perception of impermanence for the conceit 'I am' will be abandoned.

FEBRUARY 28

❋

The killing of anger with its poisoned root
and honeyed tip
This is the killing that the noble ones praise,
For having slain that, one does not sorrow.

MARCH 1

❋

Just as the great ocean has one taste, the taste of salt,
so also this Dharma and Discipline has one taste, the
taste of liberation.

MARCH 2

*

Rain soddens what is covered up,
It does not sodden what is open.
Therefore uncover what is covered
That the rain will not sodden it.

MARCH 3

❋

Practice according to Dharma,
One enjoying the Dharma,
And delighting in the Dharma,
Reflecting upon the Dharma,
Does not fall from the Dharma.

MARCH 4

❋

Whether walking or standing,
Sitting or lying down,
With mind inwardly restrained,
He attains to lasting peace.

MARCH 5

*

Even though one might hold on to the hem of my clothes and follow close behind me step by step, if he is envious, negative, corrupt in thought, unmindful, uncomprehending, unconcentrated, of wandering mind and uncontrolled faculties, he is far from me and I am far from him.

What is the reason? Such a person does not see the Dharma. Not seeing the Dharma, he does not see me.

MARCH 6

*

He should so investigate that as he investigates, his consciousness is not distracted and diffused externally. Internally he is not fixed. By not grasping anything one remains undisturbed.

By not grasping anything, there is no coming into existence of birth, ageing, death and suffering in the future.

MARCH 7

✺

Joy is non-attachment for one who is content
Joy is for one who has practised Dharma and sees
Joy is non-affliction in this world
Joy is the overcoming of sensual desires
The abolition of the conceit 'I am'
– that is truly the supreme joy.

MARCH 8

❋

If there were no gratification in the world, beings would not become attached to the world. But as there is gratification in the world, beings become attached to it.

If there were no danger in the world, beings would not become disenchanted with the world. But as there is danger in the world, beings become disenchanted with it.

If there were no way out from the world, beings could not escape from the world. But as there is a way out from the world, beings can escape from it.

MARCH 9

❈

Victory begets arrogance, the defeated dwell in pain.
Happily the peaceful live, discarding both victory
and defeat.

MARCH 10

❋

Hunger is the worst disease, conditioned things the worst suffering. Knowing this as it really is, the wise realise Nirvana, the highest bliss. Health is the highest gain and contentment the greatest wealth. A trustworthy person is the best relative.

MARCH 11

✴

One develops the four bases for spiritual power due to meditative concentration through intention, energy, state of mind and investigation.

Having developed and cultivated the bases for spiritual power, one enters and dwells in the taintless liberation through wisdom.

＊

From attachment springs grief, from attachment springs fear. For him who is wholly free from attachment there is no grief, whence then fear?

MARCH 13

＊

Whatever in the world is found in sensual pleasures
And whatever there is of heavenly bliss,
These are not worth a sixteenth part
Of the bliss of craving's destruction.

*

One follows things that should not be followed and does not follow things that should be followed. It is because one does this that unwished for, undesired, disagreeable things increase and wished for, desired, agreeable things diminish.

    Why is that? This is what happens to one who does not see.

MARCH 15

✳

Suppose there were a hen with eight or ten or twelve eggs, which she had covered, incubated, and nurtured properly. Even though she did not wish: 'Oh, that my chicks might pierce their shells with the points of their claws and beaks and hatch out safely!' yet the chicks are capable of piercing their shells with the points of their claws and beaks and hatching out safely.

So too, when a noble student has virtue... he is called one in higher training who has entered upon the way. His eggs are unspoiled; he is capable of breaking out, capable of enlightenment and attaining the supreme security from bondage.

MARCH 16

❋

Rahula, whoever in the past purified their bodily, verbal and mental actions, did so by repeatedly reflecting on their actions.

Whoever in the future will purify their bodily, verbal and mental actions will do so by repeatedly reflecting thus.

Whoever in the present is purifying their bodily, verbal and mental actions does so through repeated reflecting.

MARCH 17

❋

Rahula, develop meditation that is like the earth; for when you develop meditation that is like the earth, arisen agreeable and disagreeable contacts will not invade your mind.

Just as people throw clean things and dirty things, excrement, urine, spittle, pus and blood on the earth, and the earth is not horrified, humiliated and disgusted because of that, so too, Rahula, develop meditation that is like the earth.

MARCH 18

✳

Be a refuge unto oneself.

❇

What have I left undeclared?

'The world is eternal' – I have left undeclared.

'The world is not eternal' – I have left undeclared.

'The world is finite' – I have left undeclared.

'The world is infinite' – I have left undeclared.

'The soul is the same as the body'
– I have left undeclared.

'The soul is one thing and the body another'
– I have left undeclared.

'After death an enlightened one exists'
– I have left undeclared.

'After death an enlightened one does not exist'
– I have left undeclared.

'After death One Thus Gone (beyond wanting and clinging) both exists and does not exist'
– I have left undeclared.

'After death One Thus Gone neither exists nor does not exist' – I have left undeclared

MARCH 20

❋

What have I declared?

'This is suffering' – I have declared.

'This is the origin of suffering' – I have declared.

'This is the cessation of suffering' – I have declared.

'This is the way leading to the cessation of suffering'
– I have declared.

MARCH 21

❋

Men, driven by fear, go for refuge to many places – to hills, woods, trees and shrines. Not by resorting to such a refuge is one released from all suffering.

He who has gone for refuge to the Buddha, the Dharma and the Sangha penetrates with wisdom the Four Noble Truths.

MARCH 22

*

One employs the speech currently used in the world without adhering to it.

MARCH 23

*

I had three palaces, one for the rainy season, one for the winter and one for the summer. I lived in the rains' palace for the four months of the rainy season, enjoying myself with musicians who were all female, and I did not go down to the lower palace.

On a later occasion, having understood as they actually are the origin, the disappearance, the gratification, the danger and the escape in the case of sensual pleasures, I abandoned the pursuit of sensual pleasures, I removed fever for sensual pleasures, and I abide without thirst, with a mind inwardly at peace.

MARCH 24

❋

What way is there the preservation of truth? How does one preserve truth?

If a person has a belief, he preserves truth when he says: 'My belief is thus'. He does not yet come to the definite conclusion: 'Only this is true, anything else is wrong'.

In this way, there is the preservation of truth.

✳

When he gives ear, he hears the Dharma. He memorises it and examines the meaning of the teachings he has memorised. When he examines their meaning, he gains a reflective acceptance of those teachings. Zeal springs up.

Having applied his will, he scrutinises. Resolutely striving, he realises with the body the ultimate truth and sees it by penetrating it with wisdom. In this way, there is the discovery of truth.

MARCH 26

❋

Form is like a lump of foam,
Feeling like a water bubble;
Perception is like a mirage,
Volitions like a plantain trunk,
And consciousness like an illusion.

MARCH 27

✳

There are three searches. The search for pleasure, the search for continued existence and the search for a spiritual life. The Noble Path is to be developed for full understanding of these three searches.

MARCH 28

✴

It is by way of elements that beings come together
and unite.
Those with faith unite with those with faith
Those concerned with wrong doing unite with those
similarly concerned
And the wise with the wise.

❋

How is there the opinion of a majority? If you cannot settle that dispute in that dwelling place, they should go to a dwelling place where there is a greater number of people. You should all meet together in concord. Then, having met together, the guideline of the Dharma should be drawn out.

Once the guideline of the Dharma has been drawn out, that dispute should be settled in a way that accords with it. Such is the opinion of a majority. And so there comes to be the settlement of some disputes here by the opinion of a majority.

MARCH 30

❋

Suppose there were a deadly poisonous snake, and a man came who wanted to live, not to die, and recoiled from pain. What do you think, would that man give that deadly poisonous snake his hand or his thumb, knowing: 'If I am bitten by him I will incur death or deadly suffering'? 'No.'

So too, when one practises restraint throughout the senses and in the mind, having understood that attachment is the root of suffering, one is without attachment.

MARCH 31

❋

Ignorance (about suffering) is impermanent, conditioned, dependently arisen, subject to destruction, vanishing, fading away and cessation.

APRIL 1

*

A young tender infant lying prone does not even have the notion 'personality', so how could personality view arise in him? Yet the underlying tendency to personality view lies within him.

A young tender infant lying prone does not even have the notion 'teachings', so how could doubt about teachings arise in him? Yet the underlying tendency to doubt lies within him.

A young tender infant lying prone does not even have the notion 'rules', so how he could adherence to rules and observances arise in him? Yet the underlying tendency to adhere to rules and observances lies within him.

APRIL 2

✳

A noble student considers thus: 'I am not anything belonging to anyone anywhere, nor is there anything belonging to me in anyone anywhere.'

APRIL 3

❋

The priest asked: 'Why is it that some of your students have reached Nirvana and some have not?'

The Buddha replied: 'Are you familiar with the road leading to Rajagaha?'

'Yes, I am familiar with the road leading to Rajagaha.'

'Suppose a man came who wanted to go to Rajagaha, and he approached you and said: "Venerable sir, I want to go to Rajagaha. Show me the road to Rajagaha." Then you told him: "Now, good man, this road goes to Rajagaha. Follow it for awhile and you will see a certain village, go a little further and you will see a certain town, go a little further and you will see Rajagaha with its lovely parks, groves, meadows, and ponds."

'Then, having been thus advised and instructed by you, he would arrive safely in Rajagaha. Now, since Rajagaha exists and the path leading to Rajagaha exists and you are present as the guide, what is the cause and reason why, when those men have been thus advised and instructed by you, one man takes a wrong road and goes to the west and one arrives safely in Rajagaha?'

'What can I do about that? I am one who shows the way.'

'So too, Nirvana exists and the path leading to Nirvana exists and I am present as the guide.'

APRIL 4

❋

With the giving up and relinquishing of clinging
to standpoints and underlying tendencies regarding
consciousness, I have understood that my mind is
liberated.

APRIL 5

❋

Here one goes to the forest or to the root of a tree or to an empty hut and sits down. Having folded his legs crosswise, set his body erect and established mindfulness in front of him, mindful he breathes in, mindful he breathes out.

APRIL 6

❋

Breathing in long, he understands: 'I breathe in long'; or breathing out long, he understands: 'I breathe out long'.

Breathing in short, he understands: 'I breathe in short'; or breathing out short, he understands: 'I breathe out short'.

He trains thus: 'I shall breathe in experiencing the whole body'; he trains thus: 'I shall breathe out experiencing the whole body'.

He trains thus: 'I shall breathe in tranquillising the bodily formation'; he trains thus: 'I shall breathe out tranquillising the bodily formation'.

✳

He trains thus: 'I shall breathe in experiencing the mind'; he trains thus: 'I shall breathe out experiencing the mind'.

He trains thus: 'I shall breathe in gladdening the mind'; he trains thus: 'I shall breathe out gladdening the mind'.

He trains thus: 'I shall breathe in concentrating the mind'; he trains thus: 'I shall breathe out concentrating the mind'.

He trains thus: 'I shall breathe in liberating the mind'; he trains thus: 'I shall breathe out liberating the mind'.

APRIL 8

❋

One reviews this same body up from the soles of the feet and down from the top of the hair, bounded by skin, as full of many kinds of impurity thus: 'In this body there are head-hairs, body-hairs, nails, teeth, skin, flesh, sinews, bones, bone-marrow, kidneys, heart, liver, diaphragm, spleen, lungs, large intestines, small intestines, contents of the stomach, faeces, bile, phlegm, pus, blood, sweat, fat, tears, grease, spittle, snot, oil of the joints and urine.'

APRIL 9

*

How does one revive the past? Thinking, 'I had such material form in the past', one finds delight in that. Thinking, 'I had such feeling in the past'. . . 'I had such perception in the past'. . . 'I had such thoughts in the past'. . . 'I had such consciousness in the past', one finds delight in that.

✳

For the One who has Gone Beyond (limitations) feelings are known as they arise, as they are present, as they disappear; perceptions are known as they arise, as they are present, as they disappear; thoughts are known as they arise, as they are present, as they disappear.

✳

How is it possible that Prince Jayasena, enjoying sensual pleasures, being devoured by thoughts of sensual pleasures, bent on the search for sensual pleasures, could know, see and realise that through letting them go? That is impossible.

APRIL 12

✳

Suppose a man needing milk, seeking milk, wandering in search of milk, were to pull a recently-calved cow by her horn. Then, if he made an aspiration or if he made no aspiration, he would still be unable to procure any milk. Why is that? Because that is not the way to procure milk. So too whoever has wrong view is unable to procure any fruit.

APRIL 13

✳

Let not a person revive the past
Or on the future build his hopes,
For the past has been left behind
And the future has not been reached.
Instead with insight let him see
Each presently arisen state,
Let him know that and be sure of it,
Invincibly, unshakeably.

APRIL 14

❋

Today the effort must be made;
Tomorrow death may come, who knows?
No bargain with mortality
Can keep him and his hordes away,
But one who dwells thus ardently,
Relentlessly, by day, by night
It is he, the Peaceful Sage has said,
Who has one auspicious night.

APRIL 15

✳

How does one build up hope upon the future? Thinking, 'I may have such material form in the future', one finds delight in that. Thinking, 'I may have such feeling in the future'. . . 'I may have such perception in the future'. . . 'I may have such thoughts in the future'. . . 'I may have such consciousness in the future', one finds delight in that. That is how one builds up hope upon the future.

*

When that material form changes and becomes different, his consciousness is preoccupied with the physical changes.

Agitated mental states born of preoccupation with such changes arise together and remain obsessing his mind. Because his mind is obsessed, he is anxious, distressed and concerned.

APRIL 17

*

For the good to do what is good is easy,
For the bad to do what is good is difficult;
For the bad to do what is bad is easy,
For the noble to do what is bad is difficult.

*

It is by discussion with a person that his or her wisdom is to be known and then only after a long time, not after a short period; and only by considering it, not without consideration; and only by one who is wise, not by a fool.

APRIL 19

*

Some monks and priests
Are deeply attached to their own views;
People who see only one side of things
Engage in quarrels and disputes.

✳

Humanity is attached to self-production
Or holds to production by another.
Those who have not understood this
Have not seen it as a dart.
One who sees clearly
Does not claim, 'I am the doer',
Nor does he claim 'Another is the doer'.
Humanity is possessed by conceit,
Fettered by conceit, bound by conceit,
Speaking vindictively because of their views.

APRIL 21

✻

Farmer Bharadvaja said: 'I plough and sow. Having ploughed and sown, I eat. You should plough and sow and then eat. But I see no yoke, nor plough, nor oxen.'

The Buddha replied: 'Confidence is the seed. Self-control is the rein. Wisdom is my yoke and plough. Mindfulness is my goad. Effort is my oxen. I make Truth the destroyer of weeds. My yoked-oxen takes me to Nirvana without stopping. Having accomplished this ploughing, one becomes free from suffering.

✳

'Who craves?'

'Not a valid question,' the Buddha replied. "Due to what condition does craving arise?" would be a valid question. To this the valid answer is: "With feeling as a condition, craving arises." With craving as condition, clinging comes to be. Such is the origin of this whole mass of suffering.'

✳

If people knew, as I know, the result of giving and sharing, they would not eat a meal without having shared it, nor would they allow the stain of meanness to obsess them and take root in their minds.

Even if it were their last mouthful, they would not eat a meal without having shared it, if there were someone to share it with.

But because people do not know, as I know, the result of giving and sharing, they eat without having given, and the stain of meanness obsesses them and takes root in their minds.

APRIL 25

*

Whatever the reasons for a fortunate rebirth, they do not equal a sixteenth part of the mind-release of loving-kindness. The mind-release of loving-kindness surpasses them and shines, bright and brilliant.

❋

There are two things that cause no remorse. What are the two? Here someone has done what is good, wholesome and beneficial. He has not done evil, callous, wrongful deeds. He is not remorseful on thinking, 'I have done good', and is not remorseful on thinking, 'I have done no evil'.

APRIL 27

❋

Where there is an arising of One Thus Gone or no arising, the intrinsic nature still persists, namely the stableness of the Dharma and particular conditionality.

One Thus Gone awakens to it and elucidates on it.

APRIL 28

❋

Those of peaceful mind, discerning,
Mindful, given to meditation,
Clearly see things rightly
And do not long for sensual pleasures.
Those peaceful ones, delighting in diligence,
Who see fear in negligence,
Are incapable of falling away
And are close to Nirvana.

APRIL 29

＊

Having seen what has come to be
As having come to be,
Passing beyond what has come to be,
They are released in accordance with truth.

*

Desire and lust for the eye is a corruption of the mind. Desire and lust for the ear, nose, tongue, body and mind is a corruption.

A mind fortified by letting go becomes wieldy in regard to those things that are to be realised by direct knowing.

MAY 1

✳

One should not pursue self-gratification, which is low, vulgar, coarse, ignoble and unbeneficial; and one should not pursue self-hatred, which is painful, ignoble and unbeneficial.

The Middle Way leads to peace, to direct knowing, to enlightenment.

MAY 2

※

There are four incomprehensibles which if obsessed about would lead to insanity and distress.

The range of (the mind) of a Buddha

The range of meditative concentration

The results of karma

Speculative views about the world

MAY 3

❋

These four things are conducive to the growth of wisdom. What four?

Association with noble persons

Hearing the good Dharma

Wise attention

Practice in accordance with the Dharma

MAY 4

❋

With an unguarded body,
And encumbered by wrong understanding,
Overcome by lethargy and boredom,
One goes along in the power of Mara.

So one should be guarded in mind,
One should make right thought one's domain,
When one has put right view to the forefront
And understood rise and fall
One overcomes lethargy and boredom.

MAY 5

I regard the eye, eye-consciousness, and things cognisable through eye-consciousness thus: 'This is not mine. This I am not. This is not my self.'

I regard the ear. . . the nose. . . the tongue. . . the body. . . the mind, mind-consciousness, and things cognisable thus: 'This is not mine. This I am not. This is not my self.'

MAY 6

✳

There is wavering in one who is dependent;
There is no wavering in one who is independent;
When there is no wavering, there is calmness;
When there is calmness, there is no bias
When there is no bias, there is no coming and going
When there is no coming and going, there is no
passing away and reappearing; when there is no
passing away and reappearing, there is no here nor
beyond nor in between. This is the end of suffering.

MAY 7

✳

Channa used the knife. He is not to be blamed.
(The Buddha's conclusion after the suicide of
Channa following his liberation.)

MAY 8

✳

Raindrops on a slightly sloping lotus leaf roll off and do not remain there.

In the same way, when equanimity is established so anything at all, agreeable, disagreeable or both, just as quickly and easily do not remain in the mind.

This is called in the Noble One's Discipline the supreme development of the mental faculties.

MAY 9

❋

Even if bandits were to sever you savagely limb by limb with a two-handled saw, he who gave rise to a mind of hate towards them would not be carrying out my teaching.

*

I declare that there are two persons one can never repay. What two? One's mother and father. Even if one should carry about one's mother on one shoulder and one's father on the other, and while doing so should live a hundred years, even by that one would not do enough for one's parents.

Even if one were to establish one's parents as the supreme lords and rulers over this earth one would not repay them.

What is the reason for this?

Parents do much for their children: they bring them up, feed them and guide them through this world.

But one who encourages his disbelieving parents, settles and establishes them in faith; who encourages and establishes his immoral parents in virtue; who encourages and establishes his stingy parents in generosity; who encourages and establishes his ignorant parents in wisdom – such a one does enough for his parents. He more than repays them for what they have done.

MAY 11

❋

There are three conditioned marks of the Conditioned. What three? Its arising is discerned, its passing is discerned, its change while persisting is discerned.

There are three unconditioned marks of the Unconditioned. What three? No arising is discerned, no passing is discerned, no change while persisting is discerned.

MAY 12

❋

Two things partake of supreme knowledge. What two? Calmness and insight.

If calmness is developed, what benefit does it bring? The mind becomes developed. And what is the benefit of a developed mind? Running after pleasure is abandoned.

If insight is developed, what benefit does it bring? Wisdom becomes developed. And what is the benefit of developed wisdom? All ignorance is abandoned.

Thus through the fading away of running after pleasure, there is liberation of mind; and through the fading away of ignorance there is liberation by wisdom.

MAY 13

❋

Some misguided people learn the Dharma discourses, verses, sayings and answers to questions – but having learned the Dharma, they do not examine the meaning of these teachings with wisdom. Not examining the meaning of these teachings with wisdom, they do not gain a reflective acceptance of them.

Instead they learn the Dharma only for the sake of criticising others and for winning in debates. They do not experience the good for the sake of which they learned the Dharma. These teachings, being wrongly grasped by them, conduce to their harm and suffering for a long time.

MAY 14

✳

Just as, with an assemblage of parts,
The word 'chariot' is used,
(though a chariot does not exist independently
of its parts)
So, when the aggregates (body, feelings,
perceptions, thoughts, consciousness) exist,
There is the convention 'a being'
(although a being does not exist independently
of its parts).

MAY 15

✳

One who is friendly amidst the hostile,
Peaceful amidst the violent and unattached
amidst the attached
– this person I call spiritual.

MAY 16

*

When walking, he understands: 'I am walking';

When standing, he understands: 'I am standing';

When sitting, he understands: 'I am sitting';

When lying down, he understands: 'I am lying down'; or he understands accordingly however his body is used.

MAY 17

❋

One understands contracted mind as contracted
mind, and distracted mind as distracted mind.

One understands exalted mind as exalted mind, and
unexalted mind as unexalted mind.

One understands surpassed mind as surpassed mind,
and unsurpassed mind as unsurpassed mind.

One understands concentrated mind as concentrated
mind, and unconcentrated mind as unconcentrated mind.

One understands liberated mind as liberated mind,
and unliberated mind as unliberated mind.

MAY 18

*

By fully understanding the form element
Without getting stuck in the formless,
They are released
And leave death far behind them.

MAY 19

✳

One who does not judge others arbitrarily, but passes judgement impartially, according to truth, that person is a guardian of the Dharma and is called 'just'.

MAY 20

＊

There are these three grounds for making merit. What three? The ground for making merit consisting in giving, the ground for making merit consisting in virtue, and the ground for making merit consisting in mental development.

MAY 21

Perceiving what can be expressed through concepts,
Beings take their stand on what is expressed.
Not fully understanding the expressed,
They come under the bondage of Death.

Understanding what is expressed,
The peaceful one delights in the peaceful state.
Standing on Dharma, clearly knowing,
One freely makes use of concepts
But no more enters into the range of concepts.

MAY 22

✳

There are these three kinds of good conduct. What are the three? Good conduct by body, good conduct by speech and good conduct by mind.

MAY 23

❇

Mindfulness is established to the extent necessary for bare knowing. So one abides independent, not clinging to anything in this world.

MAY 24

❋

Whatever person one befriends,
Whomever one associates with,
One becomes of like quality,
One becomes like one's companion.

MAY 25

❋

I have shown you how the Dharma is similar to a raft, being for the purpose of crossing over, not for the purpose of grasping.

When you know the Dharma is similar to a raft, you should abandon even good states, how much more bad states.

MAY 26

❋

How does personality view come to be? Here an untaught ordinary person, who has no regard for noble ones and is unskilled and undisciplined in their Dharma, regards the body as self, or self as possessing a body, or the body is in the self or the self is in the body.

He regards feelings, perceptions, thoughts and consciousness in the same way.

MAY 27

＊

Those dyed in their desires, wrapped in darkness
Will never discern this abstruse Dharma
Which goes against the worldly stream,
Subtle, deep and difficult to see.

MAY 28

*

One has realised here and now through direct knowing that unequalled goal of the spiritual life, for the
sake of which children from good families rightly go
forth from home to the homeless state.

MAY 29

❋

While still young, a black-haired young man endowed with the blessing of youth, in the prime of life, though my mother and father wished otherwise and wept with tearful faces, I shaved off my hair and beard, dressed as a renunciate and went forth from the home life into homelessness.

MAY 30

✳

This generation delights in worldliness, rejoices in it. It is hard for such a generation to see this truth, namely the conditions for dependent arising of phenomena.

It is hard to see this truth, namely, the stilling of all formations, the relinquishing of all attachments.

MAY 31

❋

The development and practice of the perception of impermanence exhausts

Desire for sensual experiences

For material forms

For becoming and ignorance

And removes self-pride

JUNE 1

From craving springs grief, from craving springs fear.
For him who is wholly free from craving there is no
grief, whence then fear?

JUNE 2

❋

People hold dear one who embodies virtue and insight, who is principled, has realised the Truth, and who himself does what he ought to be doing.

JUNE 3

❋

What has weighed down everything?
What is most extensive?
What is the one thing that has
Everything under its control?

Naming has weighed down everything
Nothing is more extensive than naming
Naming is the one thing that has
All under its control.

JUNE 4

✳

Thinking himself a lion, the jackal says:
'I'm the king of beasts' and tries to roar
A lion's roar but only howls instead
Lion is lion and jackal jackal still.

JUNE 5

❋

One is not versed in Dharma because one speaks much. One who, after hearing even a little Dharma, does not neglect it but personally realises its truth, is truly versed in the Dharma.

JUNE 6

✳

Of all paths the Eightfold Path is the best; of all truths the Four Noble Truths are the best; of all people one who sees clearly is the best.

You yourselves must strive; the Buddhas only point the way. Those meditative ones who tread the path are released from the bonds of Mara.

All conditioned things are impermanent. When one sees this with wisdom one turns away from suffering.

JUNE 7

❊

Those who are speculators about the past, the future or both, have fixed views. Such views are merely the feeling of those who do not know and see. They experience these feelings by repeated contact with impressions on the senses and in the mind. These feelings condition desire. Desire conditions clinging (to these speculations).

JUNE 8

✳

All conditioned things are unsatisfactory. When one sees this with wisdom one turns away from suffering.

All things are not self – when one sees this with wisdom one turns away from suffering.

JUNE 9

✳

Wisdom springs from meditation,
without meditation wisdom wanes.

Having known these two paths of progress and
decline, let a person so conduct himself that his
wisdom may increase.

JUNE 10

❋

I understand Nirvana, and the path and way leading to Nirvana. I also understand how one who has entered this path will abide in liberation of mind by wisdom by realising for himself through direct knowing, here and now.

JUNE 11

*

On taking refuge in his home from a heavy monsoon, Dhaniya said: 'I dwell near the bank of the river. My house is thatched, the fire is kindled. Rain, O cloud, if you like.'

The Buddha replied: 'I abide near the river bank. My house (body) is uncovered. The fire of desire has gone out. I have passed over the floods to Nirvana.

'I have no use of a raft (teachers, teachings, practices). For a long time, my mind has been trained. I am no one's servant. Rain, O cloud, if you like.'

JUNE 12

*

Suppose a man were wounded by an arrow thickly smeared with poison, and his friends and companions, his kinsmen and relatives, brought a surgeon to treat him. The man would say 'I will not let the surgeon pull out this arrow until I know whether the man who wounded me was a priest, businessman or worker.

'I will not let the surgeon pull out the arrow until I know the name, height, skin colour, town or whether he used a long bow or crossbow and what kind of feathers he used and wood for the arrow.'

All of this would not be known to the man so he would die. If anyone should say 'I shall not lead the spiritual life until the Buddha declares to me whether the world is eternal or whether the One Thus Gone exists or not after death', that would remain undeclared and meanwhile the person would die.

JUNE 13

❋

What is dependent arising? With birth as condition, ageing-and-death comes to be: whether there is an arising of One Thus Gone (beyond desire) or no arising of such a person, that element still persists, namely specific conditionality.

One Thus Gone awakens to this and breaks through it. Having done so, he explains it and teaches it.

❋

I do not dispute with the world. The world disputes with me. A proclaimer of the Dharma does not dispute with anyone in the world. What is not believed by the wise in the world, of that I say, 'it is not so'. What is believed by the wise in the world, of that I say 'it is so'.

JUNE 15

*

I will teach you Totality. Listen, attend carefully to it and I will speak. Now what is the Totality? It is just the eye and the visible objects, the ear and sounds, the nose and smell, the tongue and tastes, the body and touch, the mind and the objects of mind. This is Totality.

Now, whoever should speak thus: 'Setting aside this Totality, I will proclaim another Totality', it would be mere talk on his part and on being questioned he would be unable to proceed and, in addition, vexation would befall him. For what reason? It would not be within his scope.

JUNE 16

❋

The wise see action as it really is. They understand how it dependently arises and are skilled in attending to action and results.

Action makes the world go round. People become bound to their actions like a chariot wheel by a pin.

JUNE 17

✳

Perceptions and notions tinged by mental proliferation beset a person. If nothing is found there to hold to, this is the end of the underlying tendency to wanting more and more, to aversion, views, doubt, conceit, becoming and ignorance.

This is the end of resorting to weapons, quarrels, brawls, disputes and revenge.

JUNE 18

*

A person of understanding knows how the senses work in relationship to the mind and the world. The person has gone beyond 'black and white' (duality) and is steadfast. Going beyond all knowledge, one is a person who knows.

JUNE 19

✳

I will teach you the end of the path (called)
The Truth
The Unaging
The Stable
The Undisintegrating
The Deathless
The Sublime
Nirvana
Freedom
The Refuge

JUNE 20

✳

What is the freedom of mind through emptiness?
One reflects thus: This is empty of self or of what
belongs to a self. Unshakeable freedom of mind
is empty of greed, hate and delusion.

JUNE 21

*

I will teach you the Dharma for the full understanding of all grasping.

Dependent upon the eye and visible objects visual consciousness arises. Contact is the coming together of these three. Conditioned by contact is feeling. So seeing, the instructed noble student is dispassionate towards the eye, is dispassionate towards objects.

Being dispassionate he is non-attached, being non-attached he is liberated. Being liberated he knows that grasping has been fully understood.

JUNE 22

❋

Supposing there were a file of blind men each in touch with the next. The first one does not see, the middle one does not see and the last one does not see. The priests seem to be like a file of blind men. That being so, does not the faith of the priests turn out to be groundless?

JUNE 23

*

Just as a cloth that is defiled and stained becomes pure and bright with the help of clear water, or just as gold becomes pure and bright with the help of a furnace, so too does one of virtue.

JUNE 24

❉

Just as a dog bound by a leash tied to a firm post or pillar keeps on running and circling around it, so too people live in fear and disgust of personality. One goes beyond that.

JUNE 25

❋

Suppose a man loved a woman with his mind bound to her by intense desire and passion. He might see that woman standing with another man chatting, joking and laughing.

Would not sorrow, pain and despair arise in that man? If he abandoned his desire and lust for her, would sorrow, pain and despair arise in him?

JUNE 26

❋

The supreme noble wisdom is the knowing of the destruction of all suffering. This freedom, founded upon truth, is unshakeable. This noble truth, namely Nirvana, has an undeceptive nature.

JUNE 27

Whatever is not yours, abandon it. When you have abandoned it, that will lead to your welfare and happiness for a long time.

What is it that is not yours? Material form is not yours. Abandon it. When you have abandoned it, that will lead to your welfare and happiness for a long time.

JUNE 28

❋

Having learned the Dharma, they examine the meaning of these teachings with wisdom. They gain a reflective acceptance of them. They do not learn the Dharma for the sake of criticising others. The teachings are conducive to their welfare and happiness for a long time.

JUNE 29

❋

A deer-trapper does not lay down bait for a deer herd intending thus: 'May the deer herd enjoy this bait that I have laid down and so be long-lived and handsome and endure for a long time.'

A deer-trapper lays down bait for a deer herd intending thus: 'The deer herd will eat food unwarily by going right in amongst the bait that I have laid down. By so doing they will become intoxicated; they will fall into negligence. I can do with them as I like on account of this bait.'

(In this analogy, 'bait' is a term for sense desire. The deer-trapper is Mara (Temptation).)

JUNE 30

✳

One walks without fear.
Stands without fear.
Sits without fear.
Lies down without fear.
Why is that? Because one is out of Mara's range.

JULY 1

❋

Not by observing silence does one become a Sage, if he be foolish and ignorant. The wise one, as if holding a balance for the scales, accepts only the good and rejects the evil. Since he comprehends both, he is called a Sage.

JULY 2

❋

Blind is this world. Here only a few possess insight. Only a few, like birds escaping from a net, go to the realms of joy. Better than sole sovereignty over the Earth, better than going to Heaven, better than lordship over all the worlds, is the fruition of a noble life.

JULY 3

*

With mind concentrated, he directs and applies his mind to the knowledge of others' minds. He knows and distinguishes with his mind the minds of other people.

JULY 4

❋

From a Dharma student: 'The Buddha has made the Dharma clear in many ways, as though he were turning upright what had been overthrown, revealing what was hidden, showing the way to one who was lost, or holding up a lamp in the dark for those with eyesight to see forms'.

JULY 5

❋

If I think and ponder upon thoughts of letting go, even for a night and day, I see nothing to fear from it. But with excessive thinking and pondering, I might tire my body, and when the body is tired, the mind might become disturbed. It is far from concentration.

So I steadied my mind and concentrated it so that it would not be disturbed.

JULY 6

✳

(A liberated one) will think whatever thought he wishes to think and he will not think any thought that he does not wish to think.

*

If I am subject to birth, ageing, sickness, death, sorrow and defilements, why should I seek that which is the same?

JULY 8

✳

Just as the footprint of any living being that walks can be placed within the elephant's footprint, so the elephant's footprint is declared the chief of them because of its great size. So too, all wholesome states can be included in the Four Noble Truths.

JULY 9

✳

One who sees dependent arising sees the Dharma. One who sees the Dharma sees dependent arising. And these five aggregates (body, feelings, perceptions, thoughts and consciousness) affected by clinging are dependently arising.

JULY 10

✳

'When you say that the body is my self, do you exercise any such power over that body as to say: "Let my form be thus; let my form not be thus"? If we have no mastery or perfect control over body, how can we call it "myself".'

'Is the body permanent or impermanent?' – 'Impermanent.'

'Is what is impermanent unsatisfactory or satisfactory?' – 'Unsatisfactory.'

'Is what is impermanent, unsatisfactory and subject to change fit to be regarded thus: "This is mine, this I am, this is my self"?'

'No.'

JULY 11

❋

When he has heard that nothing is worth clinging to, he directly knows everything; having directly known everything he fully understands everything.

Contemplating this, he does not cling to anything in the world. What has to be done has been done. There is no more becoming.

JULY 12

✳

There has never been found a fire which intends, 'Let me burn the fool', but a fool who assaults a fire burns himself by his own doing.

JULY 13

❋

One does not see in unwholesome states the danger,
degradation and defilement.

JULY 14

✳

Speculative views are a thicket, a wilderness, beset by suffering and by fever, and do not lead to enlightenment.

One Thus Gone (beyond views) is liberated from reckoning in terms of consciousness. One is profound, immeasurable, unfathomable like the ocean.

JULY 15

✳

Shrouded in darkness, why don't you seek the light?

JULY 16

❋

There are four summaries:

Any world is unstable, it is swept away,
Has no shelter and no protector.
One has to leave all and pass on,
It is incomplete and cannot be satisfying.

JULY 17

❋

All things get rooted in the will
All things come to actual existence through
attention
All things arise from contact
All things meet in feelings
The foremost of all things is meditative
concentration.
All things are mastered by awareness
Wisdom is the peak of all things
Liberation is the essence of all things.
All things merge in the Deathless
Nirvana is the completion of all things.

JULY 18

*

I undertake the training precept to restrain from
killing breathing things
I undertake the training precept to abstain from
taking what is not given
I undertake the training precept to abstain from
causing sexual harm
I undertaking the training precept to abstain from
speaking lies
I undertake the training precept to abstain from
heedlessness due to intoxicants

JULY 19

❋

This is the Deathless, namely, the liberation of the mind through not clinging.

JULY 20

❋

What kind of acquisition of view causes unwholesome states to increase and wholesome states to diminish?

There is nothing given (to others)
Nor anything offered
Nor personal sacrifices made
Nor belief in the results of good or bad actions.

JULY 21

❊

For in whatever way they conceive of anything, the
fact is ever other than that.

JULY 22

❋

Just as a line drawn on water with a stick will quickly vanish and will not last long; even so is human life like a line drawn on water. It is short. For none who is born can escape death.

JULY 23

✳

It can be expected that one (of Dharma practice) enters upon and abides in the deliverance of mind that is temporary or the freedom that is perpetual and unshakeable.

JULY 24

These six things rarely appear in the world:

Rare in the world is the appearance of
One Thus Gone (beyond desire).

Rare in the world is the appearance of one who
teaches the Dharma and Discipline proclaimed by
One Thus Gone.

Rare in the world is it to be reborn in the land of the
noble ones.

Rare in the world is the possession of unimpaired
physical and mental faculties.

Rare in the world is absence of stupidity and
dullness.

Rare in the world is a desire for wholesome
qualities.

JULY 25

❋

Said Pingiyani: Just as a capable physician might instantly cure a patient who is in pain and gravely ill; so too, dear sir, whatever one hears of Gautama's Dharma, be it discourses, mixed prose, explanations or marvellous accounts, one's sorrow, grief and despair will vanish.

JULY 26

✳

If one can find a worthy friend, then walk with him, content and mindful. If one finds no worthy friend, then as a king leaves his conquered realm, walk in the woods alone.

Better to walk alone than with fools.

JULY 27

For one who is virtuous and endowed with virtue, there is no need for an act of will so that non-remorse arise in me. It is a natural law that non-remorse will arise in one who is virtuous.

For one free of remorse, there is no need for an act of will so that gladness will arise in me. It is a natural law that gladness will arise in one who is free from remorse.

❋

One directly knows Nirvana as Nirvana.
One does not conceive of oneself as one with
Nirvana.
One does not conceive of oneself as in Nirvana.
One does not conceive of oneself apart from
Nirvana
Why is that? So that one may fully understand it.

JULY 29

❋

I will teach you the Dharma for the full understanding of all grasping.

Dependent upon the eye and visible objects visual consciousness arises. Contact is the coming together of these three. Conditioned by contact is feeling. So seeing, the instructed noble student is dispassionate towards the eye, is dispassionate, towards objects etc.

Being dispassionate he is non-attached, being non-attached he is liberated, being liberated he knows that grasping has been fully understood.

JULY 30

❋

Friends, who declare before me that they have attained the final knowledge of arahantship, all these do so in one of four ways. What four?

One develops insight followed by calmness so the path arises within.

One develops calmness followed by insight so the path arises within.

One develops calmness and insight together.

One develops and cultivates that path, and while doing so problems are abandoned and the underlying tendencies eliminated. So there comes a time when the mind becomes internally steadied, composed, unified and concentrated.

Who declare they have attained the final knowing of arahantship, all these do so in one of these four ways.

❋

The other person is given to anger and revenge and he is firmly attached to his views. I cannot make that person emerge from the unwholesome and establish him in the wholesome. One should not underrate equanimity towards such a person.

AUGUST 1

✻

Meditating on the not-beautiful should be cultivated
for overcoming lust;
Loving kindness should be cultivated for
overcoming negativity;
Mindfulness of breathing should be cultivated for
cutting off (discursive) thinking;
The perception of impermanence should be
cultivated for the removal of the conceit 'I am'.

AUGUST 2

❋

While still an unenlightened bodhisattva,
I searched the four quarters of the universe
with my mind
And found no one dearer to me than myself.
So likewise each person is to himself most dear.
Who loves oneself can never harm another.

AUGUST 3

❋

Having slain mother (craving), father (conceit), two warrior kings (duality) and destroyed a country (sense organs and sense objects) together with its treasurer (attachment and lust), ungrieving goes the spiritual person.

AUGUST 4

❋

Those students of Gautama always awaken happily who day and night constantly practise the recollection of the Buddha.

Those students of Gautama always awaken happily who day and night constantly practise the recollection of the Dharma.

Those students of Gautama always awaken happily who day and night constantly practise the recollection of the Sangha.

AUGUST 5

✳

Those students of Gautama always awaken happily
whose minds by day and night delight in the practice
of non-harming.

AUGUST 6

❋

Those students of Gautama always awaken happily
whose minds by day and night delight in the practice
of meditation.

AUGUST 7

❋

What is clinging? There are these four kinds of clinging:

Clinging to pleasure

Clinging to views

Clinging to rules, techniques and vows

Clinging to self

AUGUST 8

❋

Let go of the past, let go of the future, let go of
the present, and cross over to the farther shore of
existence. With mind wholly liberated, you shall
come no more to birth and death.

AUGUST 9

❋

To teach the Dharma to others one should set up in oneself five standards for doing so. What five?

I shall give a gradual discourse in that way the Dharma should be taught to others.

I shall give a well-reasoned discourse.

Moved by sympathy I shall speak.

Not for the sake of worldly advantage, I shall speak.

Without alluding to myself or to others, I shall speak.

It is not easy to teach the Dharma to others. When doing so one should set up in oneself these five standards.

AUGUST 10

❋

For one who is a Dharma student
There is no other thing so helpful
For reaching the highest goal
As the factor of wise attention.

AUGUST 11

✳

He for whom there is neither this shore nor the other shore, nor yet both, he who is free of cares and is unfettered – him do I call a spiritual person.

AUGUST 12

*

Some declare the self to be:

> Material and limited
>
> Material and unlimited
>
> Immaterial and limited
>
> Immaterial and unlimited

Having seen the attraction and the peril in such views, one is freed without attachment. This is to be liberated by wisdom.

AUGUST 13

✳

This world is subject to torment;
Afflicted by contact, it calls a disease 'self'.

AUGUST 14

❋

Whoever has said that freedom from becoming comes about through some kind of becoming, none of them, I say, are free from becoming.

Whoever has said that escape from becoming comes about through non-becoming, none of them, I say, have escaped from becoming.

This suffering arises dependent upon clinging. With the ending of all grasping, no suffering is produced.

AUGUST 15

❋

Said Ananda: Half of this spiritual life is friendship with the good, companionship with the good, association with the good.

The Buddha replied: Do not say that, Ananda. The whole of this spiritual life is friendship with the good, companionship with the good, association with the good.

One who is a friend cultivates and seriously practises the Noble Eightfold Path.

AUGUST 16

❋

The streams of tears that we have shed as we journey through this existence, through being united with the disagreeable and separated from the agreeable, is more than the water in the great oceans.

AUGUST 17

✳

Trivial thoughts, subtle thoughts,
Mental jerkings that follow one along:
Not understanding these mental thoughts,
One runs back and forth with wandering mind.

But having known these mental thoughts,
The ardent and mindful one restrains them.
An awakened one has entirely abandoned them,
These mental jerkings that follow one along.

AUGUST 18

*

Unattached to things that arouse attachment,
Unangered by things that provoke anger,
When his mind is cultivated thus
How can suffering come to him?

AUGUST 19

*

For the good to do what is good is easy,
For the bad to do what is good is difficult;
For the bad to do what is bad is easy,
For the noble to do what is bad is difficult.

AUGUST 20

*

For you who enjoy living at home with the encumbrance of children, making use of sandalwood from Varanasi, wearing garlands and scents, handling gold and silver, it is difficult for you to know whether or not someone is fully liberated or whether they have entered the path to being fully liberated.

AUGUST 21

✳

Just as a solid rock is not shaken by the storm, even
so the wise are not affected by praise or blame.

AUGUST 22

*

One should not be another's man.
One should not live depending on another,
One should not make a business of Dharma.

AUGUST 23

❋

With mind concentrated, purified, clear and established, he directs and inclines it towards knowing and seeing. And he knows: This my body is material, made up from the four great elements, born of mother and father, fed on rice and gruel, impermanent, liable to be injured and abraded, broken and destroyed, and this is my consciousness which is bound to it and dependent on it.

AUGUST 24

❋

All tremble at violence, all fear death. Putting oneself
in the place of another, one should not kill nor cause
another to kill.

AUGUST 25

❊

All conditioned things are impermanent
All conditioned things are unsatisfactory
All conditioned things are not self
(not I, not myself)

AUGUST 26

✳

Behold this Dharma hard to comprehend
Here the unwise are bewildered
For those with blocked minds it is obscure
Sheer darkness for those who do not see.

Who else apart from the noble ones
Are able to understand this state (of liberation)?
When they have rightly known that state
They are fully quenched.

AUGUST 27

＊

Before long, alas! this body will lie upon the earth,
unheeded and lifeless, like a useless log.

AUGUST 28

✳

Whatever harm an enemy may do to an enemy, or a hater to a hater, an ill-directed mind inflicts on oneself a greater harm.

AUGUST 29

❋

Realising that this body is like froth, penetrating its mirage-like nature, and plucking out Mara's flower-tipped arrows, go beyond sight of the King of Death!

❋

The fool worries, thinking, 'I have sons, I have wealth'. Indeed, he does not own a self. How could he own sons? How could he own wealth?

AUGUST 31

✳

Eating, drinking, chewing and savouring end in excrement and urine; this is their outcome.

SEPTEMBER 1

❋

And what is the diversity of suffering? There is intense suffering and moderate suffering. There is suffering that fades away slowly and suffering that fades away quickly.

SEPTEMBER 2

✳

There is that base where there is no earth, no water, no fire, no air; no base consisting of infinite space, infinite consciousness, infinite nothingness; neither-perception-nor-non-perception; neither this world nor another world nor both.

Here I say there is no coming, no going, no staying, no deceasing, no arising. Not fixed, not movable, it has no support. Just this is the end of suffering.

SEPTEMBER 3

*

To arouse energy one reflects 'let the flesh and blood dry up in my body but I will not stop until I have attained what can be attained'.

The lazy person dwells in dissatisfaction, soiled by unhealthy states of mind and great is the personal good that he or she neglects. Arouse your energy. Thus you should train yourselves. Strive with diligence.

SEPTEMBER 4

✹

The one who only takes for himself can be seen to be
a false friend for four reasons.

He takes everything,

He wants a lot for very little,

What he must do he does out of fear,

He seeks his own ends.

SEPTEMBER 5

❋

What use is there for a well
If there is water everywhere?
When craving's root is severed
What should one go about seeking?

SEPTEMBER 6

✳

On seeing a visible object with the eye, one does not grasp at its major signs or secondary characteristics. Because greed and sorrow, unskilled states, would overwhelm one.

So he practises guarding it, he protects the eye-faculty, develops restraint. He experiences within himself the blameless joy that comes from maintaining this guarding of the faculties.

SEPTEMBER 7

❋

And when he knows that these five hindrances have left him, gladness arises in him, from gladness comes delight, from the delight in his mind his body is tranquillised. With a tranquil body he feels joy, and with joy his mind is concentrated.

SEPTEMBER 8

❋

The gift of Dharma excels all gifts.
The taste of Dharma excels all tastes.
The delight in Dharma excels all delights.

SEPTEMBER 9

❋

Who is called 'prosperous'?

One who cultivated the seven factors for enlightenment, namely:

Mindfulness
Enquiry
Energy
Joy
Calmness
Meditative Concentration and Equanimity.

Such a person is called prosperous.

SEPTEMBER 10

❋

With mind concentrated, he applies and directs his mind to the knowledge of others' minds.

He knows and distinguishes with his mind the minds of others.

He knows the mind with passion to be with passion.

He knows the mind without passion to be without passion, the mind with hate and the mind without hate.

SEPTEMBER 11

❋

This world for the most part depends upon a duality of existence and non-existence.

For one who sees the arising of the world as it really is with wisdom, there is no notion of non-existence in regard to the world.

For one who sees the cessation of the world as it really is with correct wisdom, there is no notion of existence in regard to the world.

SEPTEMBER 12

❋

Just as if a mighty trumpeter were with little difficulty to make a proclamation to the four quarters, so by this meditation, by this liberation of the heart through loving-kindness, he leaves nothing untouched, nothing unaffected in the sensuous sphere.

SEPTEMBER 13

✳

In this matter, those who say one's perceptions arise and cease without cause or condition are totally mistaken.

Why is that? One's perceptions arise and cease owing to a cause and conditions.

SEPTEMBER 14

❋

To hear those who have morality, meditative concentration, wisdom, liberation, knowledge and insight of liberation is of great profit.

One living mindfully considers with wisdom, investigates and undertakes an inquiry into the Dharma. At that time the enlightenment factor of inquiry is aroused.

SEPTEMBER 15

*

How does one engage in clear comprehension? Feelings are known as they arise, stay and come to an end. Thoughts are known as they arise, stay and come to an end. Perceptions are known as they arise, stay and come to an end.

One should live mindful and with clear comprehension. This is our instruction to you.

SEPTEMBER 16

✳

When one has good friends,
And is reverential and respectful,
Doing what one's friends advise,
Clearly comprehending and mindful,
One may progressively attain
The destruction of all problems.

SEPTEMBER 17

❋

It is the rule that when a buddha-to-be has entered his mother's womb, his mother by nature becomes virtuous.

It is the rule that when a buddha-to-be has entered his mother's womb, she cannot be overcome by a man with lustful thoughts.

It is the rule when the buddha-to-be issues from his mother's womb, angels welcome him first, then humans.

SEPTEMBER 18

✼

Feeling conditions craving,
Craving conditions seeking,
Seeking conditions acquisition,
Acquisition conditions decision-making,
Decision-making conditions desire,
Desire conditions attachment,
Attachment conditions appropriation,
Appropriation conditions possessiveness,
Possessiveness conditions guarding of possessions,
and so arises the taking up of evil and
unskilled states.

✸

One who says: 'Feeling is my self' should be told: 'There are three kinds of feeling, friend: pleasant, painful and neutral. Which of the three do you consider to be self?'

When a pleasant feeling is felt, no painful or neutral feeling is felt, but only pleasant feeling.

When a painful feeling is felt, no pleasant or neutral feeling is felt, but only painful feeling.

And when a neutral feeling is felt, no pleasant or painful feeling is felt, but only neutral feeling.

SEPTEMBER 20

❋

O house-builder, you are seen! You will not build this house again. For your rafters are broken and your ridgepole shattered. My mind has reached the Unconditioned: I have attained the destruction of craving.

SEPTEMBER 21

✳

I hope that you are all living in concord, with mutual appreciation, without disputing, blending like milk and water, viewing each other with kindly eyes.

SEPTEMBER 22

✳

Material form is impermanent, feeling is impermanent, perception is impermanent, thoughts are impermanent, consciousness is impermanent.

SEPTEMBER 23

✳

Our livelihood shall be purified, clear and open, flaw-
less and restrained, and we will not laud ourselves
and disparage others on account of that purified
livelihood.

SEPTEMBER 24

✳

When you say thus: 'Feeling is my self', do you exercise any power over that feeling as to say: 'Let my feeling be thus; let my feeling not be thus'?
'No.'

SEPTEMBER 25

❋

We will be moderate in eating. Reflecting wisely, we will take food neither for amusement nor for intoxication nor for the sake of physical beauty and attractiveness, but only for the endurance and continuance of this body, for ending discomfort and for assisting the spiritual life.

SEPTEMBER 26

※

With the divine eye, one sees beings passing away and reappearing, inferior and superior, fair and ugly, fortunate and unfortunate, and one understands how beings pass on according to their actions.

Just as though there were two houses with doors and a man with good sight standing there between them saw people entering the houses and coming out and passing to and fro.

SEPTEMBER 27

❋

Just as if there were a lake in a mountain recess, clear and undisturbed, so that a man with good sight standing on the bank could see shells, gravel and pebbles, and also shoals of fish swimming about and resting.

So too, one understands as it actually is: This is suffering, the origin, the cessation and the way.

SEPTEMBER 28

❋

(The Buddha) teaches the Dharma good in the beginning, good in the middle and good in the end, with the right meaning and phrasing, and he reveals a spiritual life that is utterly perfect and pure.

SEPTEMBER 29

*

The footprints of all living beings that walk fit into the footprint of the elephant.

So too, all the steps that lead to enlightenment, the faculty of wisdom is declared to be their chief.

SEPTEMBER 30

❋

If one encounters the Dharma and discipline and develops loving-kindness, compassion, appreciative joy and equanimity and finds internal peace, then that person practises the proper way.

OCTOBER 1

❋

Pleasant feeling is impermanent, conditioned, neutral dependently-arisen, bound to decay, to fade away, to cease – and so too are painful feeling and feelings – neither pleasant nor unpleasant.

So anyone who, on experiencing a pleasant feeling, thinks: 'This is my self', must, at the cessation of that pleasant feeling, think: 'My self has gone!' and the same with painful feelings or feelings neither pleasant nor unpleasant.

Whoever thinks: 'Feeling is my self' is contemplating something in this present life that is impermanent, a mixture of happiness and unhappiness, subject to arising and passing away. Therefore it is not fitting to maintain: 'Feeling is my self'.

OCTOBER 2

❋

When they want to cross the sea, the lake or pond, people make a bridge or raft – the wise have crossed already.

OCTOBER 3

❋

The mind imbued with wisdom becomes completely free from the corruptions, that is, from the corruption of sensuality, of becoming, of false views and of ignorance.

OCTOBER 4

*

Enter upon and abide in pure, supreme Emptiness.

OCTOBER 5

❋

Mindfulness is simply established to the extent necessary for bare knowing and mindfulness. One abides independent, not clinging to anything in the world.

OCTOBER 6

❋

A noble student has unwavering confidence in the Buddha.

A noble student has unwavering faith in the Dharma, thus: Well-proclaimed by the Buddha is the Dharma, visible here and now, timeless, inviting inspection, leading onward, to be comprehended by the wise each one for himself. A noble student has unwavering confidence in the Sangha, thus: Well-directed is the Sangha of the Buddha's students, of upright conduct, on the right path.

The Sangha has morality dear to the Noble Ones, unbroken, uncorrupted, conducive to meditative concentration and is liberating.

OCTOBER 7

❋

I have taught the Dharma making no 'inner' and 'outer'. The One Thus Gone has no 'teacher's fist' in respect of teachings.

If there is anyone who thinks: 'I shall take charge of the order', or 'The order should refer to me', let him make some statement about the order, but I do not think in such terms.

OCTOBER 8

❋

Ripe in years. My life-span is determined.
Now I go from you.
Be untiring, mindful, disciplined,
Guarding your minds with well-collected thought.
He who, tireless, keeps to the Dharma and discipline,
Leaving birth behind will put an end to woe.

OCTOBER 9

It may be that you will think: The teacher's instruction has ceased. It should not be seen like this, for what I have taught and explained to you as Dharma and discipline will, at my passing, be your teacher.

OCTOBER 10

❋

There are six dangers attached to addiction to strong drink and sloth-producing drugs.

Waste of money

Increased quarrelling

Liability to sickness

Loss of good name

Indecent exposure of what one eays and does

Weakening of intellect

OCTOBER 11

❋

Do not die filled with longing. To die filled with
longing is painful.

❈

Magha asked: 'I make donations, I give financial support. I am an approachable person and open to requests. The wealth I give away I made quite lawfully. Do these donations produce merit for me?'

The Buddha replied: 'These gifts and offerings are certainly worthwhile and do produce great merit. In the enjoyment of meditation, in the fullness of knowledge, in the strength of mindfulness, people find full enlightenment and are a shelter for many. When the time comes for giving gifts, these are the people to give to.'

OCTOBER 13

✳

Mind precedes all mental states. Mind is their chief; they are all mind-wrought. If a person speaks or acts with an impure mind, suffering follows him as the wheel follows the foot of the ox.

Mind is their chief; they are all mind-wrought. If with a pure mind a person speaks or acts, happiness follows him like his never-departing shadow.

OCTOBER 14

❋

Those who mistake the unessential to be essential and
the essential to be unessential, dwelling in mistaken
thoughts, never arrive at the essential.

OCTOBER 15

✳

Just as the rain breaks through an ill-thatched house, even so inflamed passion penetrates an undeveloped mind.

OCTOBER 16

❋

Much though he recites the sacred texts, but acts not accordingly, he does not partake of the blessings of a spiritual life. That heedless man is like a cattle farmer who only counts the cows of others.

OCTOBER 17

*

Wisdom and consciousness, friend – these states are conjoined, not disjoined, and it is impossible to separate each of these states from the other in order to describe the difference between them.

For what one wisely understands, that one cognises, and what one cognises, that one wisely understands.

OCTOBER 18

*

Unification of mind is meditative concentration.

OCTOBER 19

✺

There are seven underlying tendencies:

desire

aversion

views

doubt

conceit

holding onto existence

and ignorance.

This path is developed for the full understanding and abandoning of these tendencies.

OCTOBER 20

*

May all beings be happy and secure!
May their hearts be wholesome!
Whatever living beings there may be:
Weak or strong, tall or middling,
Short or large, without exception;
Seen or unseen, dwelling far or near,
Already born or yet to be born,
May all beings be happy!

One should cultivate an unlimited loving mind
Without obstruction, anger or opposition
To the whole world
Above, below and across.

One does not repeat elsewhere what one has heard in order to divide. One reunites those who are divided, a promoter of friendships, who enjoys concord, rejoices in concord, delights in concord, a speaker of words that promote concord.

Abandoning harsh speech, one abstains from harsh speech;
One speaks such words as are gentle, pleasing to the ear and loveable.
One speaks such words as go to the heart, are courteous, desired by many and agreeable to many.
Abandoning gossip, one abstains from gossip.
One speaks at the right time.
Speaks what is fact.
Speaks on what is good.
Speaks on the Dharma and the Discipline at the right time.
One speaks such words as are worth recording, reasonable, moderate and beneficial.

OCTOBER 22

❋

Heat is generated and fire is produced from the friction of two fire-sticks, but when the sticks are separated the heat then ceases and subsides.

So with the cessation of painful contact, the corresponding feelings can cease and subside.

OCTOBER 23

✳

Desire is a maker of measurement
Hate is a maker of measurement,
Delusion is a maker of measurement.
The freedom of mind that is unshakeable is
empty of measurement.

OCTOBER 24

❊

I do not perceive any single hindrance other than
the hindrance of ignorance. Obstructed through
ignorance, humankind wanders on for a long time.

OCTOBER 25

❋

Live enjoying seclusion
Mindful, given to meditation
Clearly see things
Delight in diligence
One is close to Nirvana

OCTOBER 26

❋

Go and travel for the welfare of the many, happiness of the many, out of compassion, for the benefit and happiness of gods and humans.

Teach the Dharma that is beneficial in the beginning, middle and end.

OCTOBER 27

❋

One turns one's mind away from those states and directs it towards the deathless element.

This is the way.

OCTOBER 28

✳

What is the diversity of karma? There is karma leading to the hells, to the animal realm, to the sphere of
ghosts, to the human world and to the heavenly
realms.

OCTOBER 29

✳

If you see your own benefit, then make the effort.

If you see another's benefit, then make the effort.

If you see benefit for both, then make the effort.

OCTOBER 30

❋

These teachings of One Thus Gone are profound, deep in meaning, transcendent and connected with Emptiness.

OCTOBER 31

❋

There are six dangers attached to gambling:

The winner makes enemies

The loser bewails his loss

One wastes one's present wealth

One's word in not trusted

One is despised by one's friends

One is not wanted in marriage

NOVEMBER 1

*

Truth is one. There is no second.

NOVEMBER 2

✳

Through seeing clearly the process of dependent arising, one abandons such uncertainties about oneself as:

Was I in the past? Was I not in the past?
What was I in the past? How was I in the past?
Having been what, what was I in the past?

Shall I be in the future? Shall I not be in the future?
What shall I be in the future? How shall I be in the future?
Having been what, what shall I be in the future?

Am I? Am I not? What am I? How am I?
Where have I come from? Where am I going?

NOVEMBER 3

❋

When one sees the benefits, it should be enough for him to establish the perception of non-self in all things without exception.

Notions of 'I' will dissolve.
Notions of 'mine' will dissolve.
One shall be endowed with uncommon knowledge.
One shall clearly understand causes and the
phenomena arisen from causes.

NOVEMBER 4

❋

Why was it said: this Dharma is for one of vigilant mindfulness, not for one of lax mindfulness? Here, one who is mindful, equipped with the keenest mindfulness and reflection; he remembers well and keeps in mind what has been said and done long ago.

NOVEMBER 5

❋

The one who is without blind faith, who knows the Uncreated, who has severed all links, who has destroyed all causes (for karma) and who has thrown out all desires – he truly is the most excellent of persons.

NOVEMBER 6

✳

Inspiring are the forests where worldly people find no pleasure. There the undemanding rejoice.

NOVEMBER 7

✹

Better than reciting a hundred meaningless verses is the reciting of one verse of Dharma, hearing which one attains peace.

NOVEMBER 8

＊

Better it is to live one day virtuous and meditative than to live a hundred years immoral and uncontrolled.

Better it is to live one day seeing the rise and fall of things than to live a hundred years without ever seeing the rise and fall of things.

Better it is to live one day seeing the Deathless than to live a hundred years without ever seeing the Deathless.

Better it is to live one day seeing the Supreme Truth than to live a hundred years without ever seeing the Supreme Truth.

NOVEMBER 9

❋

Think not lightly of evil, saying, 'It will not come to me'. Drop by drop is the water pot filled; likewise, the fool, gathering it little by little, fills himself with evil.

Think not lightly of good, saying, 'It will not come to me'. Drop by drop is the water pot filled; likewise, the wise person, gathering it little by little, fills himself with good.

NOVEMBER 10

❋

There are five ways teachers minister to their students:

They give thorough instruction

Make sure they have understood what needs to be understood

Give them a thorough grounding in all the necessary skills

Recommend their students to others

Enable them to feel secure.

NOVEMBER 11

If the hand has no wound, one may even carry poison in it. Poison does not affect those free from wounds. Evil does not affect those who carry no evil.

NOVEMBER 12

✳

Neither in the sky nor in mid-ocean, nor by entering into mountain clefts, nowhere in the world is there a place where one may escape from the results of evil deeds.

NOVEMBER 13

✳

In a grove of trees, the Buddha took up a few leaves in his hand and said: 'What do you think is more numerous? These few leaves that I have taken up in my hand or those in the grove overhead?

'The leaves taken up in the hand are few, but those in the grove overhead are numerous.

'So too, the things I have directly known but have not taught you are numerous, while the things I have taught you are few. And why have I not taught those many things? Because they are irrelevant to the fundamentals of the spiritual life, not leading to direct knowing of enlightenment.

'And what have I taught? I have taught: "This is suffering; its causes, its cessation and the way leading to its cessation." And why have I taught this? Because this is beneficial, relevant to the fundamentals of the spiritual life, to peace, to enlightenment and Nirvana.'

NOVEMBER 14

＊

What is the diversity of feelings?

There are pleasant feelings that are worldly or
spiritual

There are unpleasant feelings that are worldly or
spiritual

There are feelings that are neither unpleasant or
pleasant that are worldly or spiritual.

A noble student knows the conditioned arising,
the diversity and outcome of feelings.

NOVEMBER 15

✳

Just as a rocky mountain is not moved by storms,
So sights, sounds, tastes, smells, contacts and ideas,
Whether desirable or undesirable,
Will never stir one of steady nature,
Whose mind is firm and free.

✴

Therefore, friends, you should train yourselves thus: though we ourselves are joined to the Dharma (Dharma-yogis), we will praise also those who are meditators. And why?

Such outstanding people are rare in the world who have personal experience of the deathless element.

And the others should train themselves thus: though we ourselves are meditators, we will praise also those who are Dharma-yogis.

And why? Such outstanding persons are rare in the world who can by their wisdom clearly understand a difficult subject.

✳

Punnaka asked, 'Why do people make offerings to priests, rulers and their God?'

The Buddha: 'People make offerings because they want to preserve their lives as they were. Their prayers, praises and offerings were all made on the basis of reward.

'But they cannot go beyond getting old (through prayers). When a person has assessed this world from top to bottom then he becomes free from its fumes and goes beyond old age.'

NOVEMBER 18

❋

A tangle inside, a tangle outside,
This generation is entangled in a tangle.
I ask you this, O Gautama,
Who can disentangle this tangle?

One established on virtue, wise,
Developing the mind and wisdom,
Who is ardent and discreet:
Can disentangle this tangle.

NOVEMBER 19

❋

The world's end can never be reached
By means of travelling
Yet without reaching the world's end
There is no release from suffering.

Therefore, truly, the world-knower, the wise one,
Gone to the world's end, fulfiller of the spiritual life,
Having known the world's end, at peace,
Longs not for this world or another.

NOVEMBER 20

*

Just as mountains of solid rock,
Massive, reaching to the sky,
Might draw together from all sides,
Crushing all in the four quarters –
So ageing and death come
Rolling over living beings –
They spare none along the way
But come crushing everything.

There's no ground there for elephant troops,
For chariot troops and infantry.
One can't defeat them by subterfuge,
Or buy them off by means of wealth.
Therefore a person of wisdom here,
Out of regard for his own good,
Steadfast, should settle faith
In the Buddha, Dharma and Sangha.

NOVEMBER 21

❋

A naked ascetic, Kassapa, asked: 'Is suffering created by oneself?'

The Buddha replied, 'Not so.'

'Is suffering created by another?'

'Not so.'

'Is suffering created by oneself and another?'

'Not so. But there is suffering. Without veering towards extremes of self and other, there is the teaching of the middle way. With ignorance as a condition, volitional formations arise leading to the whole mass of suffering.'

NOVEMBER 22

❋

Having traversed all quarters with the mind,
One finds none anywhere dearer than oneself.
Likewise, each person holds himself most dear;
Hence one who loves himself should not harm
others.

✳

Freedom of mind of loving kindness has inner
beauty as the highest
Freedom of mind of compassion has infinite
space as the highest
Freedom of mind of appreciative joy has infinite
consciousness as the highest
Freedom of mind of equanimity has no-thingness
as the highest.

NOVEMBER 24

*

By what is the world led around?
The world is led around by the mind.

NOVEMBER 25

❋

Feelings (including emotions) should be known. The conditions and causes for feelings should be known, their diversity and their outcome as well.

NOVEMBER 26

✳

I shall teach you the Unconditioned and the way leading to the Unconditioned.

NOVEMBER 27

❋

What are the four causes of evil from which one refrains?

Evil springs from attachment, ill-will, folly and fear.

✳

One who truly sees suffering also sees the causes of suffering, sees the cessation of suffering and the way leading to the cessation of suffering.

One who truly sees the causes of suffering also sees suffering, the cessation of suffering and the way leading to the cessation of suffering.

One who truly sees the cessation of suffering also sees suffering, the causes of suffering and the way leading to the cessation of suffering.

One who truly sees the way leading to the cessation of suffering, sees suffering, the causes of suffering and the cessation of suffering.

*

When this noble student has made his mind free of hatred, free of ill will and uncorrupted, he has won these assurances in this very life.

If there is another world, and if good and bad deeds bear fruit and yield results, it is possible that with the break-up of the body after death, I shall arise in a good destination, in a heavenly world.

If there is no other world, and if good and bad deeds do not bear fruit and yield such results, then here in this very life, I live happily, free of hatred and ill will.

NOVEMBER 30

*

It's only dissatisfaction that comes to be,
Dissatisfaction that arises and falls away.
Nothing but dissatisfaction comes to be,
Nothing but dissatisfaction ceases.

DECEMBER 1

*

There are three ways of making merit. What three?
There are ways of making merit by giving, by virtue
and by the development of meditation.

DECEMBER 2

❋

I see no other thing that is so quickly transformed as the mind.

DECEMBER 3

*

For it is a sign of growth in the Discipline of the Noble One that one recognises one's offence, makes amends for it according to the rule, and in future practises restraint.

DECEMBER 4

❋

The Sangha (upholders of the Dharma) is fit for gifts, hospitality, offerings, respect and is an incomparable field of merit for the world.

DECEMBER 5

❋

Not the sweet smell of flowers, not even the fragrance of jasmine, blows against the wind. But the fragrance of virtuous people pervades all directions through the fragrance of their virtue.

DECEMBER 6

✳

You are the owner of your deeds
Heir of your deeds
Having deeds as your parents
Deeds as your family
Deeds as your refuge
You will become heirs of whatever you do.

DECEMBER 7

❉

As soon as meditative concentration has been developed by you and frequently practised, then you should train thus:

I will develop freedom of mind for loving kindness and compassion.

DECEMBER 8

✳

It is good
To abide from time to time in perceiving the
non-beautiful in the beautiful
To abide from time to time in perceiving the
beautiful in the non-beautiful.
For what reason to see the non-beautiful in the
beautiful?
So that no lust arises in me.
For what reason to see the beautiful in the
non-beautiful?
So that no hate arises in me.
For what reason should one overcome the beautiful
and non-beautiful?
So that one remains mindful, with clear
comprehension and equanimity.

DECEMBER 9

*

There are five ways of getting rid of a grudge. What five?

If a grudge arises towards any person, then one should cultivate loving-kindness, compassion or equanimity towards him.

Or one should pay no attention to him and give no thought to him. In that way one can remove the grudge.

Or one may apply to that person the fact of ownership of karma: 'This worthy person is the owner of his actions and the heir of his actions; whatever he does, good or bad, he will be heir to that.'

DECEMBER 10

✳

The tears and anguish that follow arguments and
quarrels, the arrogance, pride, grudges and insults
that go with them, are all the result of one thing. They
come from holding things precious and dear.

DECEMBER 11

❋

When he thinks of letting go, giving up, he feels an urge towards this and inclines to it, his mind is well directed. Then his mind rises above this pursuing of pleasure, ill will, violence, material things and obsession with personality.

DECEMBER 12

＊

When thinking of material things, he feels no urge towards them, nor dwells on them so that he rises above such thinking.

When thinking of renunciation and letting go, he feels an urge towards this so that his mind is well directed and well developed.

Through elimination of conceit around such matters, he puts an end to problems.

DECEMBER 13

❋

What is the gain unsurpassed? Some gain a child, a wife, wealth, this or that; or else they gain faith in an ascetic or priest of wrong views. I say it is not gain.

It is gain that is unsurpassable for purification, for passing beyond sorrow and despair, for the destruction of suffering and grief.

DECEMBER 14

There are three causes for the arising of karma. Greed is a cause for the arising of karma. Hatred is a cause for the arising of karma. Delusion is a cause for the arising of karma.

It is not non-greed that arises from greed. It is greed that arises from greed.

It is not non-hatred that arises from hatred. It is hatred that arises again from hatred.

It is not non-delusion that arises from delusion. It is delusion that arises from delusion.

DECEMBER 15

❋

The Dharma is directly visible, immediate, inviting
one to come and see, worthy of application, to be
personally experienced by the wise.

DECEMBER 16

❋

The Venerable Sumana addressed the Buddha:

An arahant, who has lived the spiritual life, has attained the goal. He has no such thought, 'There is none better than I; there is none who is equal; there is none worse.'

The Buddha said: 'It is in such a way that noble ones declare final understanding. So there is no illusion of self.'

'Yet there are some foolish persons who (mistakenly) declare that they have attained such understanding. But afterwards distress befalls them.'

DECEMBER 17

❋

A priest asks: 'What is a householder's aim?'

'Wealth is a householder's aim, his quest is for knowledge, his mainstay is his craft, his desire is for work and his ideal is to bring his work to an end.'

DECEMBER 18

✴

The Buddha: 'Tell me, when in earlier days you lived at home, were you not skilled in playing the lute?' – Sona replied 'Yes.'

'And, when the strings of your lute were too taut, was your lute well tuned and easy to play?' – 'No.'

'And when the strings of your lute were too loose, was your lute well tuned and easy to play?' – 'No.'

'When the strings of your lute were neither too taut nor too loose, but adjusted to an even pitch, was your lute then well tuned and easy to play?' – 'Yes.'

'Similarly, if energy is applied too forcefully it will lead to restlessness, and if energy is too lax it will lead to lassitude. Therefore, keep your energy in balance, penetrate to a balance of these spiritual faculties.'

DECEMBER 19

❈

It is volition that I declare to be karma. Having willed, one produces karma through body, speech or mind.

DECEMBER 20

＊

There are the blessings in realising the fruit of stream-entry (transformation to a noble life):

One is firm in the Dharma.
One is unable to fall back.
One has set a limit to suffering.
One is endowed with uncommon knowledge.
One has clearly understood causes and the
phenomena arising from causes.

DECEMBER 21

❋

A noble student thus endowed will think: No fear do I have for my livelihood. Why should I have fear about it? Have I not the four powers of wisdom, energy, unblemished life and acting benevolently?

It is one who is foolish, lazy, blameworthy and whose conduct in deeds, words and thoughts lacks benevolence who might have fear for his livelihood.

DECEMBER 22

*

There are eight ways of giving. One gives:

Spontaneously;

Out of fear;

Because of thinking, 'He too has given me a gift';

Because of thinking, 'He will give me a present, too';

Thinking that it is good to give;

Thinking, 'I cook, but they (being ascetics) do not';

Thinking, 'By giving such a gift, I shall earn a good
reputation';

Or one gives because it ennobles the mind.

DECEMBER 23

✳

Virtuous ways of conduct have non-remorse
as their benefit and reward.
Non-remorse has gladness as its benefit and reward.
Gladness has joy as its benefit and reward.
Joy has serenity as its benefit and reward.
Serenity has happiness as its benefit and reward.
Happiness has meditative concentration as its
benefit and reward.
Meditative concentration has knowing and seeing
things as they really are as its benefit and reward.
Knowing and seeing things as they really are has
non-attachment as its benefit and reward.
Non-attachment has liberation as its benefit
and reward.
In this way, virtuous ways of conduct lead
step by step to the highest.

DECEMBER 24

✴

The person of little learning (about the truth of life) grows old like a bull. He grows only in the size of his body but his wisdom does not grow.

DECEMBER 25

*

What are the blessings of loving-kindness?

If the liberation of the mind by loving-kindness is developed and cultivated, frequently practised, made one's vehicle and foundation, firmly established and properly undertaken, eleven blessings may be expected. What eleven?

One sleeps peacefully;

One sees no bad dreams;

One is dear to human beings;

One is dear to non-human beings;

One will be protected by angels;

One will feel protected from fire and poison;

One will not feel hurt by weapons;

One's mind becomes easily concentrated in meditation;

One's facial complexion will be serene;

One will die unconfused;

If one does not penetrate higher, one will be reborn in a Divine abiding.

DECEMBER 26

✳

Just as a young man or woman on viewing the image of his or her face in a bright clean mirror would know if there was a spot or no spot, so too, I have proclaimed to my students the way to understand an unliberated mind as unliberated and a liberated mind as liberated.

DECEMBER 27

❋

Ananda to the Buddha: 'Half of the spiritual life is good friendship and good companionship.'

'Not so, Ananda. This is the entire spiritual life, namely good friendship and good companionship.

'When one has a good friend and a good companion, it is to be expected that one will develop and cultivate the Noble Eightfold Path.'

DECEMBER 28

❋

The Kalamas said to the Blessed One:

'There are some ascetics and priests who come to Kesaputta. They explain their own teachings but disparage the teachings of others. For us, there is perplexity and doubt as to who speaks the truth and who speaks falsehood.'

The Buddha said: 'It is fitting for you to be perplexed.'

Do not go by oral tradition,
by lineage,
because it has been widely stated,
by a collection of scriptures,
because it is logical and reasonable,
by inference and drawing conclusions,
because it has been thought out
by acceptance of a theory,
by the seeming competence of a speaker,
or because you think, 'This is our teacher'.

But when you know for yourselves, those things censured by the wise which if undertaken and practised lead to harm and suffering, then you should abandon them.

DECEMBER 29

❋

Just as a dewdrop on the tip of a blade of grass will quickly vanish at sunrise and will not last long, so human life is like a dewdrop. It is limited and brief. This one should wisely understand.

DECEMBER 30

*

Discourse on the Qualities of a True Brahmin

*

Sonadana said:

Gautama, (the Buddha) while youthful, went from the household life into homelessness leaving his parents weeping with tear-stained faces. He is handsome, virtuous, well-spoken, the teacher's teacher of many. He has abandoned sensual desires and dispelled vanity. He teaches action and the way of action, honouring the blameless way of life.

He is a wanderer of high birth. He is a wanderer from a wealthy family. People come to consult him from kingdoms and foreign lands. Many thousands have taken refuge with him.

He is consulted by the chief of the various leaders of sects. Indeed King Seniya Bimbisara of Magadha has gone for refuge to him together with his son, his wife, his followers and his ministers. However much I might praise Gautama, that praise is insufficient, he is beyond all praise.'

DECEMBER 31

❋

Discourse on the Buddha's Last Days

❋

I declare to you: all conditioned things are of a nature
to decay – work out your liberation with diligence.
(Last words of the Buddha.)

Glossary

This is a brief definition of various words and terms used in the context of the quotations.

Arahantship: full knowing of liberation and nothing left to work on in oneself that can cause suffering.

Attachment: clinging to pleasure, views, rituals and oneself. Freedom means the end of such attachments, not the end of kindness, compassion and connection.

Becoming: constantly going on to something different or wanting to become something different. 'Becoming' refers to what has become now or what will or might become in the future and the self's relationship to becoming.

Bodhisattva: a Buddha-to-be, one who lives with deep compassion and aspires to complete enlightenment.

Bondage: losing oneself in particular situations until one sees a way out.

Buddha: literally, an Awakened One.

Consciousness: the inner factor of the mind that enables us to be a conscious human being.

Conditioned: causes and factors that affect any aspect of existence and produces change whether we like it or not.

The Deathless: synonym for Nirvana and a Freedom that death cannot take away.

Delusion: includes confusion, fantasies, fears, getting caught up in self-image etc.

Dependent arising: e.g. a motorcar depends upon numerous parts that are dependently arising together for it to be called a car. 'Dependently arising' applies to everything and everyone.

Desire: wanting for experiences, things etc that grips the mind.

Dharma: teachings of the Buddha, the Truth, duty, the nature of things.

Discipline: to follow and apply the Dharma to one's daily life.

Emptiness: means absence of any real inherent substance to phenomena due to dependent arising. Synonym for 'Freedom'. Emptiness implies the Inexpressible and Inconceivable. Emptiness makes everything possible.

Enlightenment: realisation of an indestructible liberation, the emptiness of the ego, a profound opening of the heart, and wise about existence.

Escape from the world: means a wise path or way out of suffering in the world.

Equanimity: the capacity to stay steady in the face of unhealthy patterns and towards pleasurable objects of desire; the capacity to stay steady in the face of painful situations or non-significant situations.

Evil: the deliberate volition to cause great suffering and pain to others.

Faculties: physical and mental features and qualities.

Form: what has shape such as body and material things.

Formations: various states of mind and thoughts that arise due to various patterns and tendencies.

Formless: space, consciousness etc.

Four great elements: i.e. earth, air, heat and liquid.

Gods: evolved spiritual beings.

Gone beyond: not trapped in the world of birth and death and events between the two polarities.

Heaven: a long but temporary period of joy and happiness.

'I' and *'mine'*: egotism, cherish of self, self-importance, self-condemnation

I am: in terms of Dharma, indicates a grasping onto a sense of self as if 'I am unique and separate from all else'.

Ignorance: literal translation is 'not knowing'. Means not seeing clearly so problems and suffering arise in our life.

Immaterial and limited: e.g., consciousness.

Immaterial and unlimited: e.g., to experience of consciousness of oneself is the consciousness of all.

Impurity (in reference to the body): literal translation is 'absence of what is beautiful'.

Karma: unsatisfactory influences from that past that make an impact on the present and generate further volitions and actions in body, speech and mind.

Knowing: indicates a profound knowing in daily life of a true and unshakeable freedom.

Mara: the force of temptation that leads to difficulties.

Material form: includes the physical body and all objects in our surroundings.

Material and limited: e.g., a state of being such as the body.

Material and unlimited: e.g., to experience oneness with everything else.

Meditative Concentration: meditation to ground oneself in the here and now, to see clearly into the nature of things, development of calm, and insight into 'I', 'me' and 'mine'.

Mind Flow: on-going habits and patterns of mind.

Nirvana: liberation from living in greed, hate and delusion. 'Nirvana' is immediately realisable here and now in the midst of life. The ultimate peace that also expresses a fulfilled and awakened life.

No coming and going: means indestructible freedom.

Noble Student or Noble One: a transformed person, who knows freedom and lives wisely.

One Thus Gone: reference to an enlightened one. Such a one has gone beyond clinging, wanting, standpoints, egotism and sense of limitation imposed by mind and body.

Practice: three-fold inner development through ethics, meditation and wisdom.

Proliferation: thinking excessively, compelling need to go over issues repeatedly.

Rebirth: the Buddha generally has accepted the doctrine of unresolved forces like waves arising in the ocean of existence. On a couple of occasions, he has adopted a provisional view of belief in rebirth.

Sangha: men and women who have realised a noble transformation.

Tangle: to be caught up in various matters.

Unbecoming, Unborn, Unconditioned, Unmade: synonyms for Liberation or True Freedom that is not made nor dependent on circumstances for its prescence. Fulfilment of the spiritual life.

Unconditioned: frequent simile for Liberation or Nirvana. Steady, sublime and unaffected in the midst of things.

Unwholesome: what causes problems for oneself and others through patterns of mind and behaviour.

Wholesome: what brings about benefits for oneself and others.

Useful Addresses

For further information about Buddhist retreat centres, write to the following organisations.

Dhamma Gruppe Schweiz
Postfach 5909
CH 3001
Bern
Switzerland
www.karuna.ch

Insight Meditation Society
1230 Pleasant Street
Barre,
MA 01005
USA
www.dharma.org/ims.htm

Gaia House
West Ogwell
Newton Abbot
Devon TQ12 6EN
England
e-mail: gaiahouse@gn.apc.org
www.gn.apc.org/gaiahouse
www.insightmeditation.org

Spirit Rock Meditation Center
PO Box 169
Woodacre
CA 94973
USA
e-mail: srmc@spiritrock.org
www.spiritrock.org

Index

February 7; DN 22 Greater Discourse on the Foundations of Mindfulness

February 8; DN 22 Greater Discourse on the Foundations of Mindfulness

February 9; DN 22 Greater Discourse on the Foundations of Mindfulness

February 10; DN 22 Greater Discourse on the Foundations of Mindfulness

February 11; DN 22 Greater Discourse on the Foundations of Mindfulness

February 12; M 41 Discourse to the Brahmins of Sala

February 13; AN V

February 14; Sn 893

February 15; Sn 951

February 16; Sn 1032/1033

February 17; Sn 1048

February 18; Sn 1076

February 19; Sn 1082

February 20; Sn 1098

February 21; Sn 1103

February 22; Sn 1119

February 23; Ud 1.1

February 24; Ud 1.2

February 25; Ud 1.9

February 26; Ud 1.10

February 27; M 62 Greater Discourse of Advice to Rahula

February 28; SN 7:1

March 1; Ud 5.5

March 2; Ud 5.5

March 3; It 86

March 4; It 86

March 5; It 92

March 6; It 94

March 7; Ud 2.1

March 8; AN III

March 9; Dh 201

March 10; Dh 203, 204

March 11; DN 26 Discourse on the Lion's Roar of the Turning of the Wheel

March 12; Dh 214

March 13; Ud 2.2

March 14; M 46 Greater Discourse on Ways of Undertaking things

March 15; M 53 Discourse on the Disciple in Higher Training

March 16; M 61 Discourse on Advice to (his son) Rahula at Ambalatthika

March 17; M 62 Greater Discourse of Advice to Rahula

March 18; Dh 380

March 19; M 63 Shorter Discourse to Malunkyaputta

March 20; M 63 Shorter Discourse to Malunkyaputta

March 21; Dh 188, 190-191

March 22; M 74 Discourse to Dighanakha

March 23; M 75 Discourse to Magandiya

March 24; M 95 Discourse with Canki

March 25; M 95 Discourse with Canki

March 26; SN 22:95

March 27; SN 45 161

March 28; SN 14:23

March 29; M 104 Discourse at Samagama

March 30; M 105 Discourse to Sunakkhatta

March 31; SN 12:20

April 1; M 64 Greater Discourse to Malunkyaputta

April 2; M 106 Discourse on the Way to the Imperturbable

April 3; M 107 Discourse to Ganaka Moggallana

April 4; M 112 Discourse on the Sixfold Purity

May 29; M 26 Discourse on the Noble
    Search
May 30; M 26 Discourse on the Noble
    Search
May 31; SN 22:102

June 1; Dh 216
June 2; Dh 217
June 3; SN 1:203
June 4; DN 24 Discourse on the
    Charlatan
June 5; Dh 259
June 6; Dh 273, 276, 277
June 7; DN1 Discourse on the Supreme
    Net: What the Teaching is Not
June 8; Dh 278, 279
June 9; Dh 282
June 10; M12 Greater Discourse on the
    Lions Roar
June 11; Sn 18–25
June 12; M 63 Shorter Discourse to
    Malunkyaputta
June 13; SN 12:20
June 14; SN 22:94
June 15; SN 35:23
June 16; M 98 Discourse to Vasettha
June 17; M 18 Discourse on the
    Honeyball
June 18; M 18 Discourse on the
    Honeyball
June 19; SN 43 14
June 20; M 43 Discourse on the Greater
    Series of Questions and Answers
June 21; SN 35:60
June 22; M 95 Discourse with Canki
June 23; M 7 Discourse on the Simile of
    the Cloth
June 24; M 102 Discourse on the Five
    and Three
June 25; M 101 Discourse at Devadaha

June 26; M 140 Discourse on the
    Exposition of the Elements
June 27; M 22 Discourse on the Simile of
    the Snake
June 28; M 22 Discourse on the Simile of
    the Snake
June 29; M 25 Discourse on the Bait
June 30; M 26 Discourse on the Noble
    Search

July 1; Dh 268
July 2; Dh 174,178
July 3; DN 2 Discourse on the Fruits of
    the Homeless Life
July 4; M 7 Discourse on the Simile of
    the Cloth
July 5; M 19 Discourse on Two Kinds of
    Thought
July 6; M 20 Discourse on the Removal·
    of Distracting Thoughts
July 7; M 26 Discourse on the Noble
    Search
July 8; M 28 Greater Discourse on the
    Simile of the Elephant's Footprint
July 9; M 28 Greater Discourse on the
    Simile of the Elephant's Footprint
July 10; SN 10:2
July 11; M 37 Shorter Discourse on the
    Destruction of Craving
July 12; M 50 Discourse on the Rebuke
    to Mara
July 13; M 60 Discourse on the
    Incontrovertible Teaching
July 14; M 72 Discourse to Vachagotta on
    Fire
July 15; Dh 146
July 16; M 82 Discourse on Ratthapala
July 17; AN X
July 18; MR 11

July 19; M 106 Discourse on the Way to the Imperturbable

July 20; M 114 Discourse on to be Cultivated and not to be Cultivated

July 21; M 113 Discourse on the True Man

July 22; AN VII

July 23; M 122 Greater Discourse on Emptiness

July 24; AN VI

July 25; AN V

July 26; M 128 Discourse on Imperfections

July 27; SN 10:2

July 28; M 1 Discourse on the Root of all Things

July 29; SN 35:60

July 30; AN IV

July 31; M 103 Discourse on What do you think about me?

August 1; Ud 4.1

August 2; Ud 5.1

August 3; Dh 294

August 4; Dh 296 –298

August 5; Dh 300

August 6; Dh 301

August 7; SN 12.2

August 8; Dh 348

August 9; AN V

August 10; It 16

August 11; Dh 385

August 12; DN 15 Greater Discourse on Origination

August 13; Ud 3.10

August 14; Ud 3.10

August 15; SN 45.2

August 16; SN 15:3

August 17; Ud 4.1.

August 18; Ud 4.4

August 19; Ud 5.8

August 20; Ud. 6.2

August 21; Dh 81

August 22; Ud 6.2

August 23; DN 2 Discourse on the Fruits of the Homeless Life

August 24; Dh 129

August 25; Dh 277–279

August 26; SN 35:136

August 27; Dh 41

August 28; Dh 42

August 29; Dh 46

August 30; Dh 62

August 31; AN V

September 1; AN VI

September 2; Ud 8.1

September 3; SN 12:22

September 4; DN 31 Discourse on Advice to Lay People

September 5; Ud 7.9

September 6; DN 2 Discourse on the Fruits of the Homeless Life

September 7; DN 2 Discourse on the fruits of the Homeless Life

September 8; Dh 354

September 9; DN 2 Discourse on the Fruits of the Homeless Life

September 10; DN2 Discourse on the Fruits of the Homeless Life

September 11; SN 12:15

September 12; DN 13 Discourse on the Way to Brahma

September 13; DN 9 Discourse on States of Consciousness

September 14; SN 46.3

September 15; SN 47.35

September 16; Iti 17

September 17; DN 14 Great Discourse on the Lineage

September 18; DN 15 Great Discourse on Origination

September 19; DN 15 Great Discourse on Origination

September 20; Dh 154

September 21; M 31 Shorter Discourse in Gosinga

September 22; M 35 Shorter Discourse to Saccaka

September 23; M 39 Greater Discourse at Assapura

September 24; M 35 Shorter Discourse to Saccaka

September 25; M 39 Greater Discourse at Assapura

September 26; M 39 Greater Discourse at Assapura

September 27; M 39 Greater Discourse at Assapura

September 28; M 41 Discourse to Brahmins of Sala

September 29; SN 48:54

September 30; M 40 Shorter Discourse at Assapura

October 1; DN 15 Great Discourse on Origination

October 2; DN 16 Discourse on the Buddha's Last Days

October 3; DN 16 Discourse on the Buddha's Last Days

October 4; M 121 Shorter Discourse on Emptiness

October 5; M 10 Discourse on the Foundations of Mindfulness

October 6; DN 16 Discourse on the Buddha's Last Days

October 7; DN 16 Discourse on the Buddha's Last Days

October 8; DN 16 Discourse on the Buddha's Last Days

October 9; DN 16 Discourse on the Buddha's Last Days

October 10; DN 31 Discourse on Advice to Lay People

October 11; DN 17 Discourse on a King's Renunciation

October 12; M 64 Greater Discourse to Malunkyaputta

October 13; Dh 1,2

October 14; Dh 11

October 15; Dh 13

October 16; Dh 19

October 17; M 43 Discourse on the Greater Series of Questions and Answers

October 18; M 44 Discourse on the Shorter Series of Questions and Answers

October 19; SN 45 174

October 20; Sn 143–151

October 21; M 41 Discourse to the Brahmins of Sala

October 22; SN 36:10

October 23; M 43 Discourse on the Greater Series of Questions and Answers

October 24; Ud 14

October 25; It 45

October 26; SN 105

October 27; M 64 Greater Discourse to Malunkyaputta

October 28; AN VI

October 29; AN IV

October 30; SN 20.7

October 31; DN 31 Discourse on Advice to Lay People

November 1; Sn 884

November 2; M 38 Greater Discourse on the Destruction of Craving

Rider books are available from all good bookshops or from TBS, tel: 01206 256 000.